Just Us Girls

A Bible Study on Being God's Girl in Middle School

Just Us Girls

A Bible Study on Being God's Girl in Middle School

HANNAH DUGGAN

CROSS
HILL
PRESS

Scripture taken from the New King James Version®. Copyright © 1982 by Thomas Nelson, Inc. Used by permission. All rights reserved.

ISBN-13: 978-0692276518
ISBN-10: 0692276513

Praise for *Just Us Girls*

"Hannah's heart for girls seeps through the pages! *Just Us Girls* points each girl, regardless of her age or circumstances to Jesus, the Anchor of her soul."

-Kelsey Erich, Youth Leader,
Calvary Chapel Honolulu

"As a senior pastor's wife I was able to see fresh ways to approach young ladies as I gained insights from Hannah. *Just Us Girls* offers big sisterly advice and practical road signs of what to expect ahead."

-Kathy Newman, Women's Ministry Leader
Calvary Chapel Windward

"This book is perfect for any junior high girl. Fast paced witty humor that will hold attention and help point them to the purpose God has for them. This book is going to be a great tool used at Calvary Chapel Bend."

-Matt and Shari Ferguson, Youth Leaders
Calvary Chapel Bend

"As a mom I found *Just Us Girls* relatable and engaging. Girls will be blessed by Hannah's been-there-done-that-and-lived-through-it narrative."

-Keren Stonebraker, Ministry Leader
South Shore Christian Fellowship

"*Just Us Girls* can really help us girls with the struggle of adolescence and our faith."

-Olivia, Age 13

"I'm so glad *Just Us Girls* talked about how we are beautiful. We forget that God made us for who we are, and we should appreciate the things that make us different."

-Tierney, Age 12

Praise for Hannah Duggan

"Hannah is a wunderkind. A prodigy. She is an up-and-comer with remarkable talent."

-Pastor Ben Courson
Applegate Christian Fellowship

"I've read *From the Flames* & found it to be a fascinating read! I was not only extremely impressed, but equally blessed by Hannah's words. The Lord's hand is upon this young lady!"

-Pastor Mike Stangel
North Shore Christian Fellowship

"I loved having Hannah as a leader because she's young and fun and always positive and she's just an amazing influence on us."

-Peyton
Age 13

"It gives me hope, knowing that there are young people, such as Miss Duggan, who truly care about spreading the truth."

-Angela
Amazon Reviewer

OTHER BOOKS BY HANNAH DUGGAN

Fiction

From the Flames: A Novel

Dear Kate: A Novel

Non-Fiction

Just Us Girls: A Bible Study on Being God's Girl in Middle School

For my middle school girls.
You inspired this book as you continually inspire me.
Keep changing the world!
I love you all!

CONTENTS

INTRODUCTION

I remember the braces.

I remember the hormones.

I remember the awkwardness. If I didn't trip over it, run into it, or stub my toe on it, I spilled it all over myself.

Lord have mercy! I remember middle school.

When I was in middle school my mom had an idea. She'd been praying for my walk with the Lord and my journey with Him. She prayed about how to help me navigate the unavoidably rocky years of middle school and high school. As she prayed she was burdened not only for my walk of faith, but for my friends' as well.

And so began the journey of a group that came to be known as "Girls' Class." It was a Performing Arts Group and a Bible study that began in the sixth grade and ended with our high school graduation. We met once a week and talked about the issues that messed with us, things that we didn't feel comfortable sharing in church, or even in youth group. We were more open and transparent because it was just us girls, being girls. Over the years we had tea parties, pizza parties, and out of town trips. That one afternoon a week became an oasis in the midst of the desert of high school, but it started in middle school. We were sweaty, hyper, hormonal kids who were desperate for attention and some mature girl time.

All girls struggle with questions at this age. They need someone to come alongside them and remind them that they're not alone and that there are plenty of other girls grappling with the same issues. That's my goal with this book. No matter where they come from or what they struggle with, girls can find a common ground in the Word of God. It speaks to their every need, whether they know it or not. I want to give them the freedom to be honest in a safe, God-honoring environment and to let them know that middle school can be some of the best years of their lives. For a girl, this season can be the crossroads when she decides what she will believe and who she will follow, and how is she to make those decisions if she has no one to talk to and no one to guide her?

I want to make this study a special experience. There are twelve chapters in this book. Each chapter is followed by five daily devotions that dig deeper into the subject discussed in the previous chapter.

If you're an individual reading this book...

It's up to you how you want to experience this. Maybe you just want to read the chapters. If that's all you have time for that's great. If you can I encourage you to do the devotions. It's one thing to see God's Word on the page. It's another to apply it to our lives, and that's what studying Scripture is all about.

If you are a Bible study leader...

You know where your group is at and how much they can commit to. I found that for my group the best routine was to read the chapters as a group, let them do the devotions over the week, and then pull discussion questions from the devotions for the following week. It was a great way to get the girls talking and hear their hearts on the subject. You can order copies of *Just Us Girls* for your study group as well as download extra study guides from my website (hannahrosed.com).

I don't know why you picked up *Just Us Girls*. You might be a girl in need of something to read. You might be a Bible study leader in need of some material. You might be a mom in need of some direction. No matter who you are, know that I have prayed for you and asked that God will use this book in your life for His glory.

Throughout high school I've seen kids walk away, leave their faith, and end up completely shipwrecked. I've also seen kids trust God, follow His leading, and live exceptional, adventurous lives for His glory. What was the difference? Often, it was issues that started in middle school.

It's one of the most pivotal times in a girl's life.
It's when she decides who she is.
It's when kids get mean and friends turn traitor.
It's when drama is unbearable and boys are...cute.
It's when she asks her reflection, "Am I beautiful?"
It's when expression becomes depression.
It's when identity is lost and dreams are shelved.
It's when her faith is challenged.
It's middle school, and I don't want her to bear it alone.

JUST US GIRLS QUIZ

Just Us Girls is designed to meet you right where you're at!
Take this fun personality quiz to find out what chapters will
be the most helpful for you!

1. *What Disney Princess are you?*
a. Mulan (*Mulan*)
b. Rapunzel (*Tangled*)
c. Ariel (*The Little Mermaid*)
d. Cinderella (*Cinderella*)

2. *What would you do with $100?*
a. Buy Clothes! Duh!
b. Ask my friends what I should do with it.
c. Save it.
d. Spend it on new sports gear!

3. *What do you do in your free time?*
a. Call my friends, watch make up tutorials, and highlight each other's hair.
b. Work out. Train hard. Raid the pantry!
c. Read my favorite novel…again, and learn a foreign language!
d. Wander around feeling bored.

4. *Your favorite music is...*
a. Deep and Uplifting
b. Upbeat and Popular
c. Loud
d. I don't really care.

5. *What famous person would you like to meet?*
a. It doesn't matter as long as they're famous.
b. Miss America
c. Do dead people like William Shakespeare count?
d. Olympic Athlete

6. *Your dream career is...*

a. In the spotlight

b. I hate this question because I don't know.

c. A Pro Athlete

d. Anything that helps people.

7. *You sense of fashion is...*

a. Fashion is stupid.

b. I don't care about what's popular. It's whatever I like.

c. Whatever is "in."

d. Not really sure, but it never seems to be what's popular.

8. *What's your biggest social struggle?*

a. Being made fun of as a "Goody-Two-Shoes, Know-It-All."

b. Drama!!!

c. Feeling rejected for not be into makeup and girly things.

d. Fitting in.

9. *When you're upset you want...*

a. Some alone time.

b. Friends that don't make a big deal about it.

c. Friends to cry with.

d. To journal your thoughts and feelings.

10. *The compliment you love to hear is...*

a. You're gorgeous!

b. You're kind!

c. You're so smart!

d. You're so tough!

ANSWERS

Okay! Time to tally up the score.
Each answer has a number next to it.
Don't worry! This isn't a graded test to see if your answers
were right or wrong.
The numbers aren't a point value, just a way to keep track.
See if you get mostly ones, twos, threes, or fours!

1. *What Disney Princess are you?*
a. Mulan (3)
b. Rapunzel (2)
c. Ariel (1)
d. Cinderella (4)

2. *What would you do with $100?*
a. Buy Clothes! Duh! (1)
b. Ask my friends what I should do with it. (4)
c. Save it. (2)
d. Spend it on new sports gear! (3)

3. *What do you do in your free time?*
a. Call my friends, watch make up tutorials and highlight each other's hair. (1)
b. Work out. Train hard. Raid the pantry! (3)
c. Read my favorite novel…again, and learn a foreign language! (2)
d. Wander around feeling bored. (4)

4. *Your favorite music is...*
a. Deep and Uplifting (2)
b. Upbeat and Popular (1)
c. Loud (3)
d. I don't really care. (4)

5. *What famous person would you like to meet?*
a. It doesn't matter as long as they're famous. (4)
b. Miss America (1)
c. Do dead people like William Shakespeare count? (2)
d. Olympic Athlete (3)

6. Your dream career is...

a. In the spotlight. (1)

b. I hate this question because I don't know. (4)

c. A Pro Athlete (3)

d. Anything that helps people. (2)

7. You sense of fashion is...

a. Fashion is stupid. (3)

b. I don't care about what's popular. It's whatever I like. (2)

c. Whatever is "in." (1)

d. Not really sure, but it never seems to be what's popular.(4)

8. What's your biggest social struggle?

a. Being made fun of as a "Goody-Two-Shoes, Know-It-All." (2)

b. Drama!!! (1)

c. Feeling rejected for not be into makeup and girly things. (3)

d. Fitting in. (4)

9. When you're upset you want...

a. Some alone time. (4)

b. Friends that don't make a big deal about it. (3)

c. Friends to cry with. (1)

d. To journal your thoughts and feelings. (2)

10. The compliment you love to hear is...

a. You're gorgeous! (1)

b. You're kind! (4)

c. You're so smart! (2)

d. You're so tough! (3)

Mostly Ones: *The Sugar and Spice Award*

You are the girly girl! Makeup, Music, and Fashion are your hobbies. You make friends easily and soar on the wings of a social butterfly. However, your delight in the frills can distract you from important things in life and the friends you make so easily are often lost to you because of drama. God is all about using your sensitivity and friendliness for His glory! Just remember that He cares about the inside more than the outside. The chapters you'll find most helpful in this book are:

- Chapter 2: *Drama: Did I Sign Up for This?*
- Chapter 3: *Best Friends For—almost—Ever*
- Chapter 4: *The Love of Your Life*
- Chapter 5: *Beauty and the Best*

Mostly Twos: *The Shimmering Excellence Award*

You are the front row straight A student! You aim to be the best at whatever you do, and you love to please people! However, you expansive knowledge and love of big words (like expansive) can come across as arrogance, and you can be overly serious at times. God gave you your personality and desire to please so that you can use your goals and intellect for His glory. Just make sure you're your first desire is to please Him and that you hang on to humility with both hands! The chapters you will find most helpful in this book are:

- Chapter 6: *Fighting Hard for Joy*
- Chapter 9: *Dream Chasers and World Changers*
- Chapter 11: *Warriors (And All the Tough Girls said, "Amen!")*
- Chapter 12: *Your Story*

Mostly Threes: *The Tough Stuff Award*

You are one tough cookie! While the other girls were playing with dollies you were headed down the soccer field. You're an MVP and a hard worker! However, your charisma and strength sometimes intimidate and push people away, making them feel weak. God loves to use tough girls like you to do tough things for His Kingdom. Just make sure that your strong will and pride don't hold you back! The chapters you'll find most helpful in this book are:

- Chapter 7: *LIFE: The Roller Coaster*
- Chapter 8: *The Adventure of a Lifetime*
- Chapter 10: *Tough Girls in a Tough World*
- Chapter 11: *Warriors (And All the Tough Girls Said, "Amen!")*

Mostly Fours: *The Unwritten Story Award*

You are the easy going friend that people love to be around. You don't take the spotlight, but encourage your friends toward their dreams. However, you are afraid to dream dreams of your own and easily become a doormat for people with big personalities. God cherishes your obedient spirit and can do so much with a girl who wants to let Him write her story. Just don't let fear, doubt, or worry keep you from trusting your Author. The chapters you will find most helpful in this book are:

- Chapter 1: *Who the Heck Am I?*
- Chapter 8: *The Adventure of a Lifetime*
- Chapter 9: *Dream Chasers and World Changers*
- Chapter 12: *Your Story*

CHAPTER 1

Who the Heck am I?

.

Before I formed you in the womb I knew you;
Before you were born I sanctified you;
I ordained you a prophet to the nations.

JEREMIAH 1:5

Finding Your Identity

A Game of Dress Up

I once heard it stated that whatever games a child plays from the extremely pivotal ages of three to four will determine their career. I don't know if that study holds any truth. But hey, when I was three and four I stayed in my room and played pretend with all of my imaginary friends. That's basically the job description of a fiction author.

As a little girl, I could spend hours with my imagination.

I starred in many careers as a toddler and by the age of five had quite the repertoire. My numerous performances on the stage of imagination included a doctor, a veterinarian, a princess, and a cheadle deer. (Yes, my in-depth acting studies included animal shows on PBS.)

The resident brother called my Voice Characterization of Barbie, "A stunningly lifelike performance…" and "A Higher Standard for all things plastic." (Or something like that. He was watching me from the front row of his crib, trying to cram both of his feet into his mouth at the time. So it's a loose translation.)

Mommy and Daddy gave my debut as an action hero two enthusiastic thumbs up.

Of course, the best part of my acting career was the costumes! I had my knee pads for when I was about to win the Toure De France as I pulled into the garage, the pink streamers on my handle bars rustling in the wind. There was the apron, for when I pulled fresh al dente pasta from my plastic play oven, and pretended to taste it, so the viewers at home could learn how to cook. And of course I modeled the princess dress that came complete with a magic wand and silver slippers that clicked against the floor just like Cinderella's.

I don't know if you were the dress up type when you were a little kid, but no matter what you did, I'll bet you did it with everything you had. Because that's what little kids do. They give it their all no matter what they're doing.

I don't think we give little kids enough credit. As much as we hate to try something new we forget that for them walking is new. Speaking is new. Laughing, gurgling, and using the privy are new. They try all of these things out of a self-confidence that we older people just can't understand.

To me there is nothing sweeter than seeing a little kid completely lost in their own world. Probably because I know how quickly those times fade. Soon they'll be over. Soon that princess will realize she's like every other girl in her grade. That action hero will come to terms with the fact that the chances are slim to none that she will ever save the world from an alien invasion. That Doctor will shudder and remove the coat when she realizes ten years of school and student loans will be required to apply that band-aid. (Or do whatever it is she thinks doctors do.) Yes, soon the game of dress up ends.

Or does it?

Who Are We?

Who have you dressed up to be this week?

Here's the thing. We think that we've grown out of dress up. We've moved on. We're older now.

We're wrong. Teens and adults alike are in a constant state of dress up.

On Sunday we debut as "Godly Girl."

On Monday we fit the part of "Responsible Daughter."

On Tuesday our career gets off to a bang as we dress the part of "Straight A Student."

On Wednesday we're the team's "Most Valuable Player."

On Thursday we wonder if laughing at that guy was the wrong acting approach to "Love Struck Heroine."

On Friday we pull off a convincing "Mature Miss" for all of the adults to see.

On Saturday we're "Social Butterfly", hoping that our performance is convincing enough to be approved by the critics; our friends.

Then the cycle begins again.

Now, I'm not saying that this is wrong, or that your cycle should look anything like this. I'm just pointing out that we become a lot of different people in the space of a week. I know it's true for me. In one week I usually wear the hat of Daughter, Sister, Writer, Worship Leader, Dance Teacher, Babysitter, and Teenager.

None of these things are bad. I love every one of them, but I know that none of them are who I really am.

So who are you?

It's a tough question, and finding the answer is what growing up is all about, but ask yourself this; Who would I be without the wardrobe department? What if we didn't have access to all of the costumes and all of the different hats that we wear? What would be left of us?

This isn't something that's easy to think about. It's one of our worst fears, but if that activity, those friends, or those grades were taken away, who would you be? Very often we dig through all of our outer costumes to find that we don't know. There's a void there where other people seem to have a confident, sparkling personality. That's why we love our labels. We love being "That Talented Musician" or "That Skilled Athlete" or even just "That Good Girl." We love fitting our roles at school, at home, and among our friends.

But here's the best part; if you don't know who you are inside, that's okay. You're right where God wants you.

I say this because if we don't know who we are yet, it means that we're a blank page inside. Think that sounds bad? Think again. "Create in me a clean heart, oh God, and renew a steadfast spirit within me." (Psalm 51:10)

While the world around you dabbles in their personality finger paint trying to conjure up something everyone will notice, we have the privilege of asking the God who paints the sunset to paint a personality inside of us.

But what if He makes me weird?! What if I tell Him to make me into who He wants me to be and then find out that He wants me to be a nerd?! What if I become one of those stuck up Christians that everyone feels judged by?!

God's not calling you to be weird. He may call you to

step out of your clique or your comfort zone, but His plan for you is a good one. How do I know? Well we're called to be like Jesus and what kind of a Person was He? *Gentle. Compassionate. Loving. Powerful.* That's who we're called to be.

So it's time for a different kind of dress up.

"Therefore be imitators of God as dear children." (Ephesians 5:1)

And that's our job description. We're supposed to be little kids! Dressing up to be like Jesus.

All That Matters

All of your life people will fling opinions at you. They will tell you what you need to look like, how you need to act, and who you need to be. Maybe they already have. Everyone has an opinion about you, but there's only one opinion that matters, and it's not even yours. It's God's. His opinion is all you need to care about. Once you know that, everything else falls into place. You won't care what anyone else thinks if you're trying to please the Lord with everything you have. When you know what He sees in you, the rest of your hang ups and insecurities and costumes suddenly fade into the background.

So what does He think of you?

Well here's what He says in His Word.

You are free (Romans 6:18).
You are wonderfully made (Psalm 139:14).
You are precious (1 Peter 1:7).
You are forgiven (1 John 1:9).
You are more than a conqueror (Romans 8:37).
You are His Daughter (Romans 8:14).

You are a New Creation (2 Corinthians 5:17).
You were chosen before you were born (Jeremiah 1:5).
You are loved (Ephesians 2:4).

In case you were wondering, that's who you are.

Chapter 1

Who the Heck am I?
Daily Study Guide

Day 1
Read 1 Corinthians 13:11

A. When you were a child what was your favorite game? Do you think that it's affected who you've become?

B. Little kids love trying new things. What is one new thing you wish you weren't afraid to try?

C. Journal a prayer asking God to give you the courage to step out and trust Him in whatever area seems new and scary.

Day 2
Read II Timothy 2:15

A. This verse shows what kind of person we're supposed to "present" ourselves as. But who are you presenting yourself *to*? God, or other people? Who are you trying to please?

B. Who have you dressed up to be this week? List seven roles that you filled this week, one for every day. (If you want to get creative, get out your colored pencils and sketch out what your "costumes" look like.)

C. Are there any roles you fill in you day to day life that feel fake, or put on? This week examine how you act and what you say. Are you putting on a show to impress other people?

DAY 3
Read Psalm 139:23-24

A. Who would you be if every *dress up* costume was taken away? If nothing was left except you and God who would you be?

B. Here's a better question: Who do you want to be? In five years, who do you want to be known as? Does the person you want to become match up with God's Word? Do you think it's what God wants for you? Ask God to search your heart and find who you are, so He can shape you into who He wants you to be.

C. Write out a list of practical ways you can be an imitator of Christ. It might be a cliché, but What Would Jesus Do? What would it look like if you were constantly trying to imitate Him?

DAY 4
Read Isaiah 62:4b

A. Have you ever had people put opinions on you, expecting you to be something, or someone you weren't? Write down your story without mentioning names, and ask that God would help you to forgive those people, and that He would show you who He wants you to be.

B. Have you ever had a bad opinion about yourself? How did that affect you?

C. Is it hard for you to believe that our Lord delights in you? Because He does! He's so in love with you!! Write out a prayer of thankfulness for Jesus' love for you, His daughter.

DAY 5
Read Jeremiah 1:5

A. If we don't know who we are, we know where to look. He formed you. He calls you by name. He knows who you are. Look up three verses from those listed below:

You are free (Romans 6:18).

You are wonderfully made (Psalm 139:14).

You are precious (1 Peter 1:7).

You are forgiven (1 John 1:9).

You are more than a conqueror (Romans 8:37).

You are His Daughter (Romans 8:14).

You are a New Creation (2 Corinthians 5:17).

You were chosen before you were born (Jeremiah 1:5).

You are loved (Ephesians 2:4).

B. Which truth about your identity is the hardest for you to believe? Do you have trouble believing that you're precious or powerful or even loved by Him?

C. Which one of these verses is the most difficult for you to believe? Write it out and carry it with you this week asking God to show you what it means and how to truly believe it.

Drama: Did I Sign Up for This?

That you also aspire
To lead a quiet life,
To mind your own business,
And to work with your own hands
As we commanded you.

1 THESSALONIANS 4:11

Dealing with Drama

Life's Elective

Did you hear what she said?

Did you know that he's going out with her, when, like, a week ago he was going out with her best friend?

People just think they can say whatever they want on Facebook! I mean, really?!

Drama. Drama. Drama. What's a girl to do? Why do our lives seem soaked in drama? Why does it seem to find us wherever we are? No matter what school we go to, church we attend, or friends we have there is always drama. It's everywhere. If life is a classroom drama is the elective. We don't remember signing up for it, but there it is day after day.

The only thing worse than a class you hate is a class you hate that you'll have to take again because you failed. And believe me, if you fail life's drama class you will take it over and over and over again until you pass. Some people never pass and their life is like one big soap opera. (Okay, maybe that's a stretch, but you get the idea.) No one wants a life like that.

So how do we keep from failing drama class? We learn from the best.

No! Wait! Don't go call the most dramatic person you know! That's not what I'm talking about! You heard me. Come back. Put the phone down.

I am talking, of course, about the Master of Drama, the Wizard of Words, the Greatest Writer of all time; William Shakespeare.

Drama: Comedy and Tragedy

No! Wait! Don't zone out and stop reading! I'm not going to lecture you with sixteenth century literature. Even though I might enjoy that, I have a feeling I would lose you. There's really only one thing you should know about Shakespearian Drama. There are two kinds: comedy and tragedy. Let me explain the difference.

Shakespearian Comedies:

1. As the name implies, they're funny. In a weird, "Thou speaketh way over my head," kind of way.

2. The plot usually involves a mix up. Someone falls in love with wrong person, or someone pretends to be someone they're not and gets in a ton of trouble.

3. Everyone has a brain full of rocks.

Shakespearian Tragedies:

1. As the name implies they're really really sad. Focused on betrayal and murder, the tragedies are a good way to get yourself depressed about mankind.

2. Everyone dies. Apparently, in the 1500's the happy ending hadn't been invented yet, because Hamlet, Macbeth, Julius Caesar, Antony, Cleopatra, Romeo, and Juliet all die.

3. Everyone has a brain full of rocks.

There you go! Shakespeare in a nutshell. (To any Shakespeare fans or English teachers reading this, I apologize profusely before you chuck this book into the Goodwill pile. I understand that I am making fun of the greatest writer of all time, and I myself have enormous respect for Shakespeare. He was a genius. Let's continue.)

As I considered the genres of Comedy and Tragedy, I realized that all of our drama falls into these categories as well.

Teen Drama Comedy:

1. It's funny, at least at first. It's the light stuff. The juicy gossip stuff. "No one gets hurt…except for them over there. Come on! Can't they take a joke?"

2. It usually starts, or ends with a mix up or misunderstanding. It started with a rumor that wasn't true, and ended with someone's feeling getting hurt.

3. Everyone involved acts like they have a brain full of rocks. (For some reason drama seems to numb our intelligence, making us say things and do things that we wouldn't do on paper.)

Teen Drama Tragedy:

1. It's sad. If not for us, it's sad for someone else. It's more than just hurt feelings. It's broken friendships. It's ruined reputations. It's just really sad.

2. It never ends well. While comedy drama can be laughed off, Tragedy drama cuts deep and leaves scars. It stings. And something, usually a friendship dies.

3. At the end we realize that everyone involved has a brain full of rocks. Including us.

Drama isn't something to play around with! It's dangerous, and painful. So why do we go back again and again?

I think our most innocent motivation is that we want to help. Even if it's not our drama, we want to be there for our friends. We want to help. Let me tell you something that's hard for girls to hear.

It's not your job to help.

Let me explain something. If you have a friend who is in serious danger, then you need to get an adult's help, but that's not what I'm talking about. I'm talking about a dramatic situation that your friend got themselves into. We all have that friend who is obsessed with drama. It seems to hover over her like a swarm of bees. And I promise you that if you are near her you will get stung. Jumping into the middle of someone else's drama is never the answer. As Paul said to the Thessalonians.

"That you also aspire to lead a quiet life, to **mind your own business**, and to work with your own hands, as we commanded you." (I Thessalonians 4:11 emphasis mine)

When you see that friend getting involved in something she shouldn't, back away. Even if we care about them, we need to let them fight their battles and learn their lessons. We can't save them from the drama if they don't want to be saved. We can keep them in prayer knowing that God can help them in ways we simply can't.

Here are some key rules that should help us to avoid drama.

1. Don't gossip. Just don't. Don't spread it. Don't listen to it. Don't stand for it. I know how it hard is, especially for us girls, but if you're the kind of person that is willing to shut down the drama, people's reputations will be saved just by your presence in a conversation.

2. Don't ever promise to keep a secret before you know what it is. Again, this is a rule that isn't easy, but conversations that start with, "Can you keep a secret?" can be dangerous. You may find yourself suddenly knowing something you didn't want to know. Now, knowing about a surprise party is one thing, but sometimes kids confide hard and scary things. It's important that your friends know that you care about them enough to tell a safe adult when they're in danger or struggling.

3. Boys. Just don't. Just…just don't. I'd say a decent percentage of girls' drama is caused by boys. Just don't go there. You have your whole life to find "The One." You will save yourself so much drama, grief, and time if you ignore the boys for now. (But that's another chapter!)

Why is it that we say we hate drama and are then surrounded by it? Whether we want to admit it or not, it's very often our fault. We're either placing ourselves in drama filled situations, or around dramatic people, or we're just being drama queens ourselves. All of us have a little dramatic flair, but you know what? The sooner we walk away from it, the sooner we can live the life that God has planned for us.

So I leave with a few final lessons from Shakespeare and Drama:

The Taming of the Drama Queen

Drama, Drama, Drama, what's a girl to do?
You didn't search for Drama, but somehow she found you
So let us take a lesson, on this cause of strife and fear
This comedy, this tragedy, from drama's Master, Shakespeare
"Be not afraid of Drama," says the Drama Queen in you
"It's all a joke. It's nothing. why make so Much Ado?
Some girls are born dramatic, some girls drama achieve,
And some have drama thrust upon them. Poor thing! You're one
of these.
So gossip, giggle, enjoy, As You Like It, have your fill."
Woe to the girl that hears these words, and takes the bitter pill
For drama has another face, a pouting, tear-stained mask
It started out as fun and games, but somehow you came in last
Stabbed in the back, And left alone, the drama's course has run its
mile
Your kingdom for a decent friend! But there are daggers in friend's
smiles.
"I hate the drama!" you proclaim. "I wish I'd never felt its touch.
I'll never be involved again." Methinks you protest too much.
If thou hatest chocolate, why doest thou shove it in thine face?
If drama is so foul to thee, why not put it in its place?
Why don't we say farewell to her? Because parting is sweet sorrow
We can only bear to walk away, until it be morrow
Then we're lured back to her trap, what fools we mortals be!
The dramatic die a thousand deaths, let it not be so with thee

Drama: Did I Sign Up for This?
Daily Study Guide

DAY 1

Read Proverbs 17:1

A. The Old Testament Equivalent of drama is "strife" or "contention." What two situations are compared in this verse? Which one is better? Why?

B. Picture a lavish room full of swishing fabrics and delectable food, but everyone there is uncomfortable and whispering about each other. Now compare that to cramming down a granola bar all by yourself. That's the comparison being made here. How important is your social life? I'm not saying you should be a hermit, but if you're surrounded by dramatic friends that can fill a house with strife, it might be time for some new friends.

C. Spend some time in prayer asking God if there is

anything you need to change in your social life. Ask Him to reveal to you how to avoid any drama or conflict that surrounds you. Be willing to hear His answer and obey if anything needs to be changed.

DAY 2
Read II Timothy 2:23

A. What two things are we told to avoid? What do these things cause?

A. Have you ever been in a heated argument that was flat out stupid? Do you ever walk away wondering why you even got involved?

B. What are some ways you can avoid foolish disputes?

DAY 3
Read Proverbs 26:20

A. What does a fire need to keep burning? What does strife need to keep spreading?

B. Talebearing is exactly what it sounds like; taking a story and spreading it. Gossip is at the heart of nearly all drama. Have you ever been hurt by gossip? Have you ever hurt someone else by gossiping? Just to be clear, gossiping isn't just spreading gossip. It's listening to it as well.

C. Search your heart for bitterness. It's easy to be angry at people who've spread stories about you, but we can't hold onto hatred. It just weighs us down and makes us unpleasant to be around. AlSo if we don't forgive others God can't flood us with the fresh forgiveness that we need every day. "And forgive us our trespasses as we forgive those who trespass against us." (Matthew 6:12)

DAY 4
Read James 3:5-6

A. What is the tongue compared to in this verse? What is it that sets the tongue on fire?

B. Fire is a great example of what our words can do. Words can set our hearts ablaze to do great things for God, or it can set fire to a friendship as we watch it burn to the ground. What do you think are the most powerful positive words you can say? What are the most powerful negative words? (Keep it clean, please.)

C. If we're going to take the gossip and the drama out of our lives we've got to replace it with something else. Make a point of saying one encouraging thing to every person you talk to today. It might be hard to think of things for some people, but it will be worth it and might even make their day!

DAY 5
Read Proverbs 28:25

A. What kind of person stirs up strife? What will happen to those who trust the Lord?

B. What part do you think pride plays in drama? Why do you think being proud is the opposite of trusting God?

C. Journal a prayer asking God to show you what areas your pride has snuck in. Ask Him, then wait in the silence of your devotion time for Him to answer you. He will. Just listen. It might not be the answer you want to hear, but He is always faithful to speak to us. So let Him grip your heart, and don't leave until you've heard His voice.

CHAPTER 3

Best Friends For—Almost—Ever

A man who has friends must himself be friendly,
But there is a friend who sticks closer than a brother.

PROVERBS 18:24

Being a Good Friend

Friendship and Knitting

I hate knitting.

There are plenty of things I can't do (play the violin, score in volleyball, and get a score higher than fifteen in Flappy Bird) but knitting is at the top of the list. I didn't give up easily, though. I sat patiently through personal lessons, well-meaning friends, and YouTube tutorials, but alas! It was not to be. I've tried. I've failed. I wanted to knit so badly, but in the end I had to give up and mourn all the potholders and doilies that could have been. Because I hate knitting. After my last attempt all I had dangling from the end of my knitting needle was what looked like a strangled piece of floss on a stick. That's when I gave up.

I'm a crochet kind a girl. Give me a crochet hook and a ball of yarn and I can whip out a blanket while debating theology and eating sushi! One hook, one strand of yarn, one goal. That's my kind of thing.

I realized that this says a lot about my personality. In my opinion, crocheting is worlds easier than knitting because knitting requires teamwork. Two needles simultaneously click-clacking together to weave an awe-inspiring labor of love. It's a beautiful art! Crocheting on the other hand is just me doing my thing without depending on teamwork of any kind.

I think most of us are that way with our projects. I'm great at any activity that requires me working on a project by myself. Thrust me into a team situation however and now I've got to deal with people and personalities and opinions!

Crocheted blankets are beautiful, but for some reason, knitted items always have more intricacy and depth to them. It's the same way with our projects and our relationships. We'll get a lot done if we work alone, but our lives won't carry the same depth.

"That their hearts may be encouraged, being **knit** together in love…" (Colossians 2:2 emphasis mine)

God doesn't want us to be crocheted Christians. He wants us to work together, being knit into the fabric of people that He uses for His glory. So what does it mean to work together? What does it mean to be a good friend?

A Girl Who Has Friends

"A man who has friends must himself be friendly, but there is a friend who sticks closer than a brother." (Proverbs 18:24)

What does it mean to be friendly? Well that takes some practical advice and some of the best practical advice can be found in the book of Proverbs. Mainly sketched out by King Solomon, this is a book dripping with wisdom. It talks about money, marriage, parenting, and…wait for it…friendship! The word friend shows up thirteen times in the book of Proverbs, and surprisingly not one of those verses talks about how to *find* a good friend. Most of them are about how to *be* a good friend. Here's the big six:

Forgiveness

"So do this, my son, and deliver yourself; for you have come into the hand of your friend: Go and humble yourself; plead with your friend." (Proverbs 6:3)

We all mess up in our friendships. We stress. We snap. We hurt feelings. Are we willing to ask forgiveness when we do? I know it isn't easy, but it's worth it to shove aside our pride, humble ourselves, and plead without friends, even if we're not entirely to blame.

Love

"A friend loves at all times and brother is born for adversity." (Proverbs 17:17)

Let's face it. We're not going to *like* our friends at all times, but we are called to *love* them at all times. That's because love is an action, not a feeling. We need to be the kind of friend that shows love, even when our friends are driving us crazy!

Grace

"He who has purity of heart and grace on his lips, the king will be his friend." (Proverbs 22:11)

Just to be clear, grace is undeserved forgiveness and favor, the kind of forgiveness that Christ shows us. We need to show it to our friends. I love the way this verse phrases it. "Grace on his lips…" It's as if we're so full of grace we're overflowing and it spills off of our lips every time we're the slightest bit offended. Who doesn't want to be friends with someone like that?

Correction

"Faithful are the wounds of a friend, but the kisses of an enemy are deceitful." (Proverbs 27:6)

Don't be weirded out by the kisses thing! A kiss on the cheek was a common greeting among friends in Solomon's day. What the verse is talking about is flattery. Enemies will lay it on thick. They'll tell you how attractive, clever, and talented you are, just so they can get close enough to earn your trust. Friends, however know when to correct you and you can trust their correction. Often, they aren't even friends in your own age group, but we all need that parent, or that youth leader who is willing to correct us. In the same way we need to be willing to gently correct that friend who's gossiping or speaking inappropriately, or flat out being rude.

Perseverance

"Do not forsake your own friend…" (Proverbs 27:10a)

Okay, this one's pretty self-explanatory. Don't be a jerk and ditch your friend. It's easy to hear that and think, "I would never!" But I think we've all done it. We're hanging out with a friend at a party. Then someone older or cooler walks in and we forsake the friend who's stuck with us because we're trying to impress the other person. There's nothing wrong with making new friends and seeking the company of older kids, but don't ditch your friend as a result!

Sharpening

"As iron sharpens iron, so a man sharpens the countenance of his friend." (Proverbs 27:17

Have you ever seen a movie where they sharpen a knife on a wheel? What happens when the knife touches the wheel? Sparks fly. Metal grates against metal. The dull edge is shaved away.

Even the closest of friends argue and find themselves at odds with one another. Surprisingly, this isn't necessarily a bad thing. No two people are going to agree all the time, and when we disagree it can be a good indicator of who we really are on the inside. When we snap, things come out of our mouths that we didn't know were there and if we're humble enough see our faults and flaws we are sharpened just like an iron knife.

A Friend Who Sticks Closer

These are the qualities of a good friend! This is the kind of friend we need to be.

But what about the lonely times? What about the times when you feel deserted and find yourself without friends? I've been there! I've had friends reject me, ignore me, and believe the lies they'd heard about me. Very few things in life hurt worse than counting a friend an enemy. Sometimes God brings restoration to that friendship. Other times, there's no way to patch it up. It can result in some very lonely afternoons and some very hurt feelings

Yet, it's in those seasons that I drew closest to the Lord. That's why I love the second half of Proverbs 18:24: "But there is a friend who sticks closer than a brother."

Jesus is that friend. He's the Perfect Friend. He meets

all the qualifications and even added one of His own.

In John chapter fifteen Jesus and His twelve closest friends went on a walk to their favorite spot, The Mount of Olives. As they walked he spoke to them about worry, prayer, peace, and love. As the stars shone above them, I wonder if His voice shook at all as He said, "Greater love has no one than this, than to lay down one's life for his friends. You are my friends…" (John 15:13) I picture his friends looking at each other in confusion, wondering if He really meant what He said about laying down His life for them. If there was any doubt in their minds it was settled the next day when Jesus was nailed to a cross for them and for you and for me. He meant every word.

Sacrifice

Sacrifice is what it means to be a good friend. And I'm not saying that you're going to be called upon to die for anybody literally. Instead, we're called to sacrifice our wants, our needs and our time, to give them the first turn and the last cookie and anything else that is hard to give. There is no greater love on earth than the love of sacrifice! There is no greater friend than a friend who loves like Jesus loves and the way we become that friend is by spending time with Him.

It's been said that you become who you hang out with.

And that's great news if you're hanging out with Jesus!

Best Friends For—Almost—Ever
Daily Study Guide

DAY 1

Read Proverbs 6:3

A. What is the verse telling us to do? What three commands are found at the end?

B. Have you ever messed up in your friendships? Have you ever needed to ask forgiveness? Did you?

C. Time for a heart checkup! Is there anyone you've wronged recently that you need to ask for forgiveness? Think carefully over the last week. Have you offended anyone, or said anything you need to apologize for? Pray and ask the Lord to bring things to your mind.

DAY 2
Read Proverbs 17:17

A. What does a friend do? What is a brother born for?

B. When is it most challenging to love your friends? Are there any friends who are particularly hard to love? Why?

C. Pick one person this week that's hard to love. Pray for them for one minute today. I'm not being figurative! A full sixty seconds. Add another minute every day. Ask the Lord to teach you how to love them at all times. Then think of ways you can show them love. How does your heart change toward them in just a week?

DAY 3
Read Proverbs 27:17

A. What process is talked about in this verse? What does it symbolize? What does it mean to be sharpened by your friend?

B. Have you ever had a painful confrontation with a friend in the past? What did you learn? How have you changed as a result?

C. Is there anyone you are being sharpened by right now? Maybe it's not someone in your circle of friends. Maybe it's a sibling or another family member. Is it hard to imagine that God could bring something good out of this difficult experience? Pray for the person that is sharpening you. Ask God to help you see the situation through His eyes. It might be painful, but sister if you let Him do His thing, He'll work it out for good. I promise.

Day 4
Read John 15:13

A. What is the greatest form of love? Who are we to lay our lives down for?

B. Has anyone ever sacrificed anything for you? (If you have a mother the answer is yes!) Who are they? What did they give up for you? How did it make you feel?

C. What are three things that you could give up for someone else? Is it your time, your resources, your desire to feel important? What are you going to give up for someone else this week? It doesn't have to be big. Little sacrifices will often go unnoticed by the one you're giving them to. Give of yourself, and God will notice every time!

Day 5
Read Proverbs 18:24

A. He who has friends must do what? How close does Jesus stick to us?

B. Which quality of friendship (forgiveness, love, grace, perseverance, sharpening, or sacrifice) is hardest for you? Why do you think that is?

C. What could you do to work on this quality? How could you become a better friend? Do you need to forgive someone? Love your enemies? Persevere in a difficult relationship? The only two people who know are you and God. So ask Him what He wants you to do to become a better friend!

CHAPTER 4

The Love of Your Life

The Lord has appeared of old to me, saying:
"Yes, I have loved you with an everlasting love;
Therefore with lovingkindness I have drawn you."

JEREMIAH 31:3

Waiting for Love

Super Charming

You're standing in a room crowded with young people. It's rather warm, bringing out that charming blush in your cheeks. Okay, let's face it. It's like a hundred and eighty degrees and you're sweating like a pig. The only consolation is that the odor wafting through the room lets you know you're not the only one. You're attempting to feel attractive, but honestly your recent growth spurt is making you feel like an ostrich in last year's dress, and you're terrified to say something stupid.

Then *he* walks up.

That guy you've been admiring across the room, the one your friends are giggling about. He steps out of the crowd, and you're sure he's come to talk to one of your friends. Then he sees you. "Hi," he says with a toss of his Beiber flip. "What's your name?"

You'd tell him if you could only remember. But it doesn't matter. He carries on an easy conversation. Within moments you know everything about him, and you feel like you've been friends for a lifetime. He's cute, chatty, and doesn't smell like a vat of toxic waste. Obviously, he is the one. If Super Man's secret identity was Prince Charming and he sang for One Direction you couldn't be more smitten. You're in love. It's that simple.

And then you wake up.

Super Charming is nowhere to be seen. You're drooling in your jammies, just you and your morning breath. Welcome to Love.

Love as Advertised on the Disney Channel

Come on, now! We've all had that dream, whether it was while you were snoozing, or enduring health class. (Or maybe you were doing both at the same time.) That perfect guy. That special someone. I like to call him Super Charming.

We look for him everywhere, at school, at church, and at the grocery store. (Or is that just me?)

We don't know what he'll look like, but he'll be perfect. The boy of our dreams.

We don't know when we'll find him, but when we do we'll just know.

He'll walk into a room and instantly be stunned by our beauty. He'll drop to one knee and say, "Hey, I just met you and this is crazy!" He'll hand you his number. You'll call him…maybe.

Nope. Sorry, ladies. As you may have noticed, these things only happen in dreams and Disney movies. We're searching for our Super Charming, and don't know where to find him because he doesn't exist.

Now, not to say that young love doesn't happen. I know plenty of couples that met in their teens. (My parents met in the sixth grade for crying out loud!) But love doesn't appear, "As advertised on the Disney Channel."

Young love is explosive. Putting a sacred and difficult thing such as romance in the hands of kids like us, is like handing us an arm load of fireworks. (Not the driveway kind. The huge kind. The explode-in-your-face-someone's-going-to-get-hurt-if-you're-not-careful kind.)

Love and fireworks are beautiful, but only if they're used correctly. If not, things blow up, and you get burned. Sadly, this is most often the case with young love.

In my honest opinion a wise girl is going to leave boys alone, until she's ready to get married. Jumping from boyfriend to boyfriend is a great way to waste your life. Those who do are just asking for heartbreak. Why?

Because teens are the most passionate people on this planet! Very few of us can love just a little. When we fall, we fall hard. Because love is a new and exciting experience we throw everything we've got into it, and then when things don't work out we find that love has an ugly evil twin; Hate.

When you fall in love again and again, have that boyfriend, pursue that crush, it might be fun. It might be wonderful to have a string of boys who go crazy for you, but in the end, they'll be a string of enemies and heartbreaks.

One of my favorite verses about love is Song of Solomon 8:4: "I charge you, oh Daughters of Jerusalem, Do not awaken, nor stir up love until it pleases."

Here's where we can go wrong with that verse. We want to stir up love when it pleases *us*. We need to wait, not stirring up love until it pleases *God*, but His timing and our timing, are usually two very different things.

True Love to Those Who Wait

So since we like to daydream, let's try something. Picture the love of your life. You haven't met him yet. Only you know what he looks like, how tall he is, and what his laugh sounds like. Don't picture someone you know. Don't even picture someone you know *of.* (Ummm, like Tim Tebow…cough cough. You know who you are.) I want you to picture your future husband. Picture that one stranger you've never met. He stands somewhere in your future, waiting to hold your heart.

Got it? Okay! Now picture him with a girl. Not you. Someone else. Another stranger. They're not just standing near each other. They're obviously together. They're not just talking. They're completely obsessed with each other. She's not just looking at him. She's making the goo-goo eyes. What's worse, he's making the goo-goo eyes back! He's talking to this girl like she's you!

Feeling betrayed yet?

What if your future husband could see you when you talk to other guys? What would he think? Would he feel betrayed? Maybe you've saved your first kiss for him, maybe you've never had a boyfriend, but when you talk to a guy what is your attitude? Would it hurt the future love of your life, if he could see you flirt with that guy? What about the way you dress? You know what? The right guy wants a girl who hasn't shown off the body God gave her to everyone at the beach.

When we have this perspective it causes us to be careful. It makes us more guarded in our speech, our actions, and our dress. Now, just to be clear there's nothing wrong with dressing cute! I love a cute pair of jeans and a V-neck as much as the next girl, but in our culture we need to think about what it means to be modest, but more of that later!

For my thirteenth birthday I received the book *When God Writes Your Love Story* by Eric and Leslie Ludy. It brought so much into perspective for me when I read it. The couple who wrote the book has an incredible heart for the Lord and a hilarious sense of humor. One of the sweetest stories in the book is about Eric Ludy. He wrote love letters to his future wife before he ever met Leslie. Then on their honeymoon, he gave her a box of letters he'd been writing for years. On that same thirteenth birthday I was given a leather journal. If you haven't figured this out yet, books are kind of my thing. So this gift could not have been bestowed on a more grateful subject. The card from a dear friend of mine said that the journal was so I could write down all of my secret feelings and crushes. A year later, the journal remained blank. Not because I didn't have those feelings, but because I didn't want to write them down. I knew my feelings and crushes would change. I pictured myself falling in love with someone and writing all about them in my journal only to have the relationship end in heart break. I knew that if that happened I'd want to burn the journal, not keep it. So on my fourteenth birthday I made a decision. I would write to my future husband, and I have. Whenever I feel discouraged, lonely, or oh so single, I write to him. Instead of fantasizing over anyone I actually know, I set my hope in the plans God has for me.

Sister, there is no better romance author than God Himself. Don't believe me? Read the book of Ruth! Sandwiched right between Judges and First Samuel, this book is one of the sweetest romances of all time, and God has an even better story planned for you.

But wait! There's more!

He's madly in love with you.

He thinks about you all day and all night.

He knows your favorite color, favorite food, and favorite movie.

He loves to make you laugh, and hates to see you cry.

He always wants to talk, and is ready to listen.

He makes you the priority.

He spends an eternity thinking of ways to romance you.

He'd lay down His life for you.

Actually, He already did.

He thought of you with His dying breath.

He stood in your place, to protect you from the trouble you got yourself in.

His love for you was so powerful that death itself couldn't hold Him.

He wrote you the Sixty-Six Book Love Letter that has changed the world.

He is madly in love with you.

Jesus Christ is what we long for.

All right, so maybe Super Charming doesn't exist. In the end, guys are human, just like us, full of flaws and shortcomings. If we expect a human's love for us to make us happy we'll come up short and disappointed every time. But there's a reason you long for someone who fits the above description. You're longing for a deeper relationship with Christ. You desire and thirst for someone who cares about you more than you can understand. Once we realize that it's God and not a guy that we long for, we find so much contentment.

Now, is there a guy out there for you? My guess is, yes

there is!

But you know what? Before you meet your fella, I encourage you to fall in love. Fall in love with Jesus Christ. Make Him the love of your life. Don't go chasing after love. "Wait on the Lord and be of good Courage! And He will strengthen your heart. Wait I say on the Lord" (Psalm 27:14). If you're doing what God has called you to do, everything else is going to fall into place, including your love story. So don't fear! Wait on the Lord. Trust in Him. It worked for Ruth. It worked for Eve. It worked for Mary. God is no stranger to love. So why not put down the fireworks, and let God bring you the love of your life in His perfect, romantic timing?

CHAPTER 4
The Love of Your Life
Daily Study Guide

DAY 1

Read Song of Solomon 8:4 (Some versions list it as Song of Songs.)

A. Who is this verse talking to? What aren't we supposed to stir up?

B. How is love advertised on TV? What are some ways that our culture stirs up love before its time?

C. Find something to remind you of your commitment to not awaken love. Maybe it's a necklace, maybe it's a bracelet, and maybe it's a purity ring. Find something that will remind you to be committed to God and carry it with you today. Do you see any changes in how your day goes?

DAY 2
Read Psalm 37:4

A. What are we to delight ourselves in? What is the result?

B. The confusion with this verse is thinking that it means God will give us whatever we want, which (Praise the Lord!) isn't true. But sometimes God has planted His desires in our hearts. (But that's another chapter!) Make a list of the desires of your heart. Then go down the list, telling God that He can choose whether or not to give you these things. Submit yourself to His will.

C. When you are struck by a desire today, ask if it's from the Lord or from your own heart. (I'm not talking about the desire for cookies.) When you think about the future and the things you want, especially if they're romantic it's important to know where that desire comes from, and give it back to Him.

DAY 3
Read Ecclesiastes 3:1

A. What two things does everything have according to this verse?

B. There is a time for everything. So I want to know what you think. When is the time fall in love? How old should you be to date? Why? I want you to tell me what the Bible says about it. Find a couple verses that talk about love and tell me what God thinks about it.

C. Take God's timing seriously. Ask Him if there are any areas where you are holding onto something and you need to let go. His timing is perfect, and if we get too set our opinions we'll miss the things He has for us right now. Ask Him if there is anything that you want that isn't for this season of your life, then wait for His answer. He will speak if you ask Him and listen.

DAY 4

Read Galatians 6:9

A. What should we not grow weary in? What will happen if we don't lose heart?

B. Being single is hard sometimes, and the enemy loves to creep in and tries to make us feel lonely or like we're going to miss out on love, but singleness is a blessing from the Lord. Tell the Lord why you are thankful for your season of life, and trust Him to hold your heart until He brings the right guy.

C. Okay, now the fun part! Write a letter to your future husband. Save it in a journal, or a box or maybe you just want to devote an entire notebook to the cause. Write him, and write prayers for him, knowing that God will bring him to you in His perfect timing.

DAY 5

Read Jeremiah 31:3

A. What kind of love has God loved us with? How has He drawn us?

B. Make a list of all the ways Jesus has romanced us and drawn us close to Him.

C. Live like you are loved! You will notice that you walk, talk, and live differently if you sincerely believe that there is a God in Heaven who is crazy about you! Every time you can today stop and remember this everlasting love with which He loves you!

CHAPTER 5

Beauty and the Best

Do not let your adornment be merely outward
—Arranging the hair, wearing gold, or putting on fine apparel—
Rather let it be the hidden person of the heart,
With the incorruptible beauty
Of a gentle and quiet spirit.

1 PETER 3:3-4

Discovering Self Worth

Story Time!

If there's anything a girl loves it's a story. Something in us particularly loves fairy tales. Maybe it's the magical words that start every story. Maybe it's the happy ending. Maybe it's the peril and the gorgeous outfits in between. The fairy tales are more than just fluffy stories we heard when we were kids. They shaped the way we think whether we realize or not. They're also very precious to my heart. I can't walk by a room where there's a Disney Princess movie playing without stopping and singing along. You're never too old for fairy tales. Which is why I've decided to tell you one. Not because I think you're little, but because I hope there is a little girl in you that still loves a good princess story. So embrace the little kid in you, and please enjoy my not-so-ancient tale; Beauty and the Best.

Once Upon a Time

Once upon a time, in a land not so far away there was a girl named Beauty. She was the loveliest citizen in the land of Girlhood. Everyone who saw her, knew that this was true without introduction. Once you met Beauty she seemed even more splendid. She had a clever sense of humor, grace in the way she carried herself, and a certain sparkle in her eyes that showed her intelligence. She was naturally kind, and lived up to her name in every way. Everyone in the Land of Girlhood knew she was lovely. Everyone, that is, except Beauty herself.

For Beauty had a nasty stepsister whose name was Body. Body had grown up in the village of Low Esteem, a frequently growing city in the Land of Girlhood. When Beauty looked in the mirror every morning Body would stand behind her and shake her head. "No, no, no," Body would sigh with the click of her tongue. "This will never do."

"What's wrong, Sister?" innocent Beauty would ask.

"It's all wrong." Making a sound of disgust, Body would stare on, disapproving.

Every morning, Beauty would endure her sister's spite and scorn, while she fixed her hair again and again. She would avoid eye contact as she applied her makeup. Then she would hold back her tears at the sight of her own reflection.

One morning as Beauty caught the reflection of her sister's glowering face in the mirror she looked at Body unable to bear her disapproval any longer. "Don't you have something better to do than watch me?" she asked.

A sly smile slid across her sister's face as she sauntered over to the mirror. "I'm just trying to help."

Beauty took a deep breath. "Well I don't need your help. I can get ready by myself."

Body laughed such a cruel and heartless laugh that Beauty wanted to shrink into herself. "You?" Body cackled. "Darling, don't you realize that I'm doing you a favor? I can't have my own stepsister walking around dressed like she doesn't know the difference between cashmere and damask."

Beauty shrunk back again. What was the difference between cashmere and damask? "The other girls in the village don't know the difference either."

Body gave a sigh. "The other girls in the village don't need as much…" She paused scrunching her face. "Help as you do. They're naturally beautiful."

"Other people have told me I'm beautiful," Beauty mumbled.

Body pursed her lips and folded her hands as if deciding on her words carefully. "Dear, do you understand that sometimes people don't really mean what they say? Sometimes they want to make you feel good and don't realize that they're making you see something that isn't really there." With these words, Body reached over and straightened the mirror hanging on the wall. Unknown to her sister, Body had learned a secret enchantment that could be cast on a mirror, until even a girl as lovely as Beauty could not look into it, without feeling ugly and ashamed. It was not an easy spell, and Body had been casting it on the mirror little by little for years. For if Beauty had noticed the change in one day, Body's plan would have been ruined. Therefore she had worked her magic here and there, tainting Beauty's view one feature at a time.

Today the enchantment had reached its peak and when Beauty gazed into the mirror the girl she saw was hideous.

Hair that couldn't be tamed, a smile that would make babies cry, and a face that no amount of makeup could ever cure.

"Can you help me, Sister?" Beauty asked, as she watched tears fall down the cheeks of her marred reflection.

"I'll do what I can," she groaned with an air of regret.

Body called for her servants, Cosmo, Holly, and Wood.

Cosmo stepped up first, a stack of magazines under his arm.

"What are those for?" asked a disappointed Beauty.

Cosmo laughed. "If you don't know what beauty looks like, how will you ever be beautiful?" He set the stack of magazines in her arms, and she sifted through them, as Body went about tangling and taking scissors to Beauty's lovely curls.

Beauty looked at the girls in the photos. They looked angry, bitter, and even frightened. "Are you sure this is what beauty looks like?" she asked.

Cosmo only laughed. "If anyone knows, it's me. Take my word for it."

Beauty didn't have a clever answer, so she did.

Holly was next. She set a laptop in Beauty's arms over the stack of magazines and pulled up several videos. The girls in the videos marched down runways looking miserable. "Do they walk like that because they're prisoners?"

Holly giggled at her simple question. "Of course not! Everyone in village of Fashion walks like that. You will too, if you know what's beautiful."

Wood started in next, blasting music through a speaker. The songs that raged through the room were all about what made a girl beautiful. The lyrics depressed her so much, that Beauty hardly noticed the way that Body transformed her. She laid on make up so thick that Beauty's face couldn't even be recognized. She cropped her hair until it was split and jagged. When at last she was done, she sighed and looked at her sister. "I'm afraid that's all I can do, Beauty."

Beauty looked in the mirror, hoping to see an image like one of the models from Cosmo's magazines. Instead she looked worse than before as she stared into the enchanted mirror.

"There's one last thing I can do for you," Body promised.

The two of them traveled to Body's home town, the city of Low Esteem. It was a miserable, filthy place filled with angry, frightened people. Beauty feared they might be robbed, or murdered in such a place, but Body strolled confidently along. This was her home.

They reached a building so tall it seemed to scrape the very sky, and they went in, traveling all the way to the top.

"Where are we going?" Beauty asked.

"To see Lord Image. He will do for you what I cannot."

Beauty was truly thankful for her sister's help, but inwardly, she was wondered why someone as important as Lord Image would condescend to see someone as ugly as her.

"My dear, there's nothing left to do for you," Lord Image puffed, waving her away with a hand weighed down with rings.

"I'll do anything," she begged. "Just please make me beautiful."

"The only people that are really beautiful are my people. My subjects. Unless you want to become one of them you will stay forever ugly."

Beauty thought of the rolling hills and pleasant

meadows in her village. She didn't want to give up all of those lovely things.

Lord Image noticed her hesitance. "I'm sorry. There's nothing I can do."

"I'll do it!" she cried.

Lord Image smiled an evil oily smile. "Very well."

Beauty turned to say goodbye to her sister. Body was smiling too, but it was a different smile. It was the smile of the winner at the end of the game. "Goodbye, Beauty," she said with the wiggle of her delicate fingers.

Lord Image commanded the guards to guide Beauty to her chambers. They dragged her back down the many stories, past the ground floor to the dungeon below.

"Let me show you to your room!" One of the guards laughed, shoving her forward. She stumbled, landing head first into the cell of self-hate.

She was not alone in the cell. Two girls she had known as children curled up in a corner and noticed her when she was thrown in. As children they had been known as Innocent, and Naïve. Now they were known as Depression and Eating Disorder. They too had been tricked by Lord Image.

"There's no way out," Depression assured her.

"We've tried everything," Eating Disorder agreed.

Beauty believed them and found her own corner in which to curl up. With nothing else to do in the quickly darkening cell, beauty traced the wall with one of her fingers. She noticed that someone had carved letters into the stone wall, and she leaned back to read them.

"I will praise You because I am fearfully and wonderfully made; Marvelous are Your works and that my soul knows very well." (Psalm 139:14)

"We've seen it," Eating Disorder moaned when she noticed Beauty staring at the words.

"It doesn't change anything," Depression added.

Beauty still stared at the words. She knew them. She'd heard them as a little girl. She remembered how her parents had taught them to her.

I'm not ugly. She thought.

The words on the wall began to glow. Or was it her imagination?

"I am beautiful," she whispered.

The words grew brighter, beginning to sputter and pop like sparks from a bonfire.

"I'm beautiful because You made me," she said out loud.

There was a cracking sound, as if the walls were splitting in two.

"You don't create ugly things."

The words were as deeply etched in her heart as they were in the stone. Suddenly there was a loud crash and the wall splintered into a thousand pieces.

Now Beauty lives a very normal life. She married and had children. She grows older every day, but does not fear age because she remembers the lesson written on the wall of self-hate.

She is not beautiful because of her looks.

She isn't beautiful because of her clever humor.

She isn't beautiful according to the world's standard.

But she is beautiful in God's sight.

And so are you.

CHAPTER 5

Beauty and the Best
Daily Study Guide

DAY 1

Read Proverbs 31:30

A. What does the verse say about charm and beauty? What is it that really matters?

B. In the story the character of Body criticized Beauty when she looked in the mirror. When you look in the mirror is there anything you feel ashamed about, or wish you could change? (Don't be afraid to be honest. You don't have to share this with the class.)

C. We all have areas of insecurity, but we need to hand them over to the Lord. Write a prayer, asking God to give you confidence, and contentment with the way He made you.

Day 2
Read 1 Peter 3:3-4

A. Where *shouldn't* we find our beauty? Where should our beauty be? What does verse four say has an "incorruptible beauty?"

B. Don't get me wrong! There's nothing wrong with arranging your hair, sporting a little bling, or some cute clothes! However, just like we talked about in an earlier lesson if we didn't have those things, who would we be? If we wore hand-me-downs, didn't own a hairbrush, or have an earring to call our own, who would we be? How important are these things to you?

C. In our culture something has been lost. "A gentle and quiet spirit." Doesn't that just sound graceful and lovely? Here's the problem; we think that means being quiet and mousy and letting everyone walk all over us. Not true. Our culture says that in order to be noticed we have to be loud and grab people's attention. Not true either. (But more on that later!) Examine your own life and ask the Lord if there are any areas where you try to draw attention to yourself instead of having the incorruptible beauty of a gentle and quiet spirit.

Day 3
Read 1 John 2:16-17

A. What three things are in the world according to verse 16? Why shouldn't we trust in those things according to verse 17? What is it that lasts forever?

B. List five ways you see the world influencing the way girls see beauty. What is the one message you think is screamed at girls the most?

C. Write how the world and the media uses each of

Satan's tools to manipulate girls today.

- ○ Lust of the Flesh
- ○ Lust of the Eyes
- ○ The Pride of Life

DAY 4

Read Genesis 1:27, 31

A. What did God create on the sixth day (v. 27)? What did He think of it (v. 31)?

B. Do you think God looks down on you and sees something "very good?" Why or why not?

C. God is perfect in His foreknowledge. When He said His creation was good He wasn't just talking about Adam and Eve. He was talking about you. Think about how He formed you, with every detail and feature of yours in mind. Every time we complain about our looks we're saying that God didn't do a good enough job creating us. He is perfect! So trust Him. Ask His forgiveness for any time you have been discontent with the way you look, or complained about the way He created you, and thank Him that all things He creates are very good!

DAY 5

Read Psalm 139:14

A. Why should we praise the Lord? What should our soul know very well?

B. Write out this verse on a 3x5 card and tape it to your mirror. Every time you fix your hair or check your reflection say the verse out loud until you have it by memory and you can say it without looking. Hopefully it will run through your head every time you look in a mirror at all.

C. If you have one available, go check out your mirror.

(A face-forward phone camera works too!) It's time for you and the Lord to have a little talk. I want you to see your reflection and repeat these words out loud. (You should wait to do this until you're alone in your room.) "You make beautiful things." Say it again, and again until you can feel His confidence within you. Because, sister, God doesn't make junk. He makes beautiful things, and He made you!

CHAPTER 6

Fighting Hard for Joy

Rejoice in the Lord always. Again I will say rejoice!

PHILIPPIANS 4:4

Rejoicing in All Things

Good Plan

"Are you ready for this day?"

"Talk to me after coffee and we'll see." That was what I told my mom first thing this morning. Why did this day seem daunting to me? For starters my cranky level is at an all-time high. Besides that, school is dragging me to the end of my rope, and I'm anxiously awaiting word on a very sick family member. What was the cherry one top? I had to write a chapter on joy today.

With no glimmer of joy I was sorely lacking inspiration. So I curled up with my coffee and my Bible. Desperate to hear from the Lord, I flipped through the pages, praying that He would speak to me in whatever verse I landed on.

"Eye has not seen nor ear has heard, nor have entered into the heart of man the things which God has prepared for those who love Him." (1 Corinthians 2:9)

Okay, Lord, what do You want to teach me about joy?

The Three Reasons

The Lord and I went on a walk. If you've never done this, you totally need to try it. Grab your headphones and your worship music, and ask Him to show you things as you take a walk with Him. Some of the best times I've ever had with the Lord have happened on our walks together.

On this particular morning I knew I needed a dose of joy, so I scrolled to my new favorite album, *The Art of Celebration* by Rend Collective. Before I bought the album a few weeks ago, I'd watched an interview with one of the band members that was so moving that I took notes as if there would be a test.

"Seriousness is not a fruit of the Spirit, but joy is." His words blew my mind. Then he went on. "There is an irrepressible laughter in the heart of God and the whole universe cannot contain it. He's the One Who invented celebrations and feasting and holidays. He is the One Who sings and dances over us."

Isn't that a great picture? Can you imagine the God of the universe seeing you and being so excited and so in love that He can't even contain His joy? He sings and dances because of His love for you that can't be held back.

Reason to rejoice number 1: God never stops rejoicing. Why should we?

But sometimes, it's not easy to rejoice. Sometimes life knocks us between the eyes, and we can't be happy. That's just it. We're never commanded to be happy in the Bible. Happiness comes along when things are going great. It's not wrong, but it's not permanent either.

We get our coffee. We're happy!

We spill our coffee. We're sad.

We're going to the movies. We're happy!

The movie stinks. We're sad.

It's Saturday. We're happy!

It's Monday. We're sad.

That's just life. Happiness is just a bonus. We live in a culture that says that we should always be happy and do whatever it is that makes us happiest, but that's the problem. Constant happiness is a lie. No one, not even Pharrell Williams is always happy! (Although his song has made many people clap along if they feel like a room without a roof…because they're haaappyyyy! Okay, so it's a good song. Sorry. Sidetrack. Moving on!) God never commands us to be happy, but He does command us to rejoice.

"Rejoice in the Lord always. Again I will say rejoice!" (Philippians 4:4)

So what's the difference? Happiness is a feeling. Joy is an action. Happiness is our response to the world. Joy is how we change the world. Happiness is that friend that sometimes calls us on weekends. Joy is the sibling that we've grown up with, share a room with, and ignore most of the time.

If we have the Holy Spirit living within us we have joy. It's that simple. It's our choice whether we take hold of it or not.

So why don't we? I think it's because we believe that real joy is irresponsible. It's unpredictable. It's not cool. Being serious makes us appear more *mature*. But if we're too mature to be joyful, then we're pretty much saying we're more mature than God. Because God created joy and commands it of us.

Reason to rejoice number 2: God said to.

I love the old fairy tale about the fisherman's wife who wished for everything she deserved. When her husband got home, they had nothing left because that's exactly what she deserved. Nothing.

It's what we deserve too. In fact, we deserve worse.

Then Jesus died, gave His life for ours, crushed Satan under His feet, and came back from the dead just because He could.

Now, instead of getting what we deserve, we're free. Instead of being guilty, we're forgiven. Instead of being punished we are blessed with grace. Instead of separation we get to spend eternity with Christ.

And I don't care if you've heard that message every day since the day you were born. It's still something to get excited about.

You know what breaks my heart? When I tell a Christian kid that, and they roll their eyes. They've heard the good news, so they shut their hearts to it.

So just think about it for a second. Hear it like you've never heard it before. Imagine that you committed a crime. It was such a bad crime that you deserved to die. Just as the judge is about to pronounce you guilty, Jesus walks into the court room and says, "I'll take her punishment. I'll stand in her place. Everything she ever did wrong goes on My record as if I did it." The judge doesn't just let you go. He makes you royalty. Suddenly you're a daughter of the King. Why would we spend one more day of our lives without joy?

"There is therefore now no condemnation to those who are in Christ Jesus." (Romans 8:1)

Reason to rejoice number 3: We're free!

Go For the Gold

As we grow up we tend to be dragged down by anger, fear, and brokenness. As the band member of Rend Collective put it, "Life has a way of draining that childlike wonder from us."

Remember when you were a little kid? Remember when little things made you laugh? When smiling was as natural as breathing? Little kids just love to laugh.

Then they grow up.

They become serious.

They lose their joy.

Middle school tends to be an age of disillusionment. Suddenly we're not little kids anymore. So we let life suck the joy right out of us, a little at a time.

Our generation is the most privileged generation to ever walk the face of the earth. Here's the sad thing. We're also the most depressed generation on the face of the earth. There are so many reason American teens are depressed, but I think one of those reasons is that we let life steal our joy.

Did you ever do any sports as a kid? If you did, you know that at the end of the year everyone gets a participation award. They're usually plastic or cheap metal. They have something written on them like, "You're the best!" Everyone gets one. Everyone's happy. Everyone's a winner. Right?

In 2012, at the London Olympics Michael Phelps stood on an Olympic podium for the nineteenth time and became the most decorated athlete in the history of the Olympic Games. Olympic Athletes don't get participation awards.

Michael Phelps, Gabby Douglas, and Apollo Ono don't get medals for just showing up. They have to train. When they're done training, they have to train some more. When they're exhausted, they have to keep going. Why? Because they want that gold medal.

Joy is a Gold Medal, not a participation award. It's there for the taking, but no one said it would be easy. We have to fight hard for it. If we want to be above average gold medal kind of Christians then we have to get training. We have to dive into God's Word. We have to talk to Him and draw near to Him. We have to let Him shave away the rough spots of our hearts until we're agile athletes for the Kingdom.

So fight hard! Don't be afraid to wrestle for your blessing, and work hard for your joy. Believe me, it's worth it! Because once we find the joy the of the Lord, no one can steal it from us.

Fighting Hard For Joy
Daily Study Guide

DAY 1

Read 1 Corinthians 2:9

   A. How does this verse make you feel? What does it have to do with joy? Have you ever seen it take place in your life?

   B. Have you ever had your frown turned upside down by the Lord? How did it happen?

   C. Journal a prayer, and surrender to God the things in your life that make you grumpy. They might be people or circumstances that you can't change. Ask the Lord to give you joy in these situations and look for His answer this week.

Day 2

Read Isaiah 62:4b

A. What delights the Lord? Do you think that your life delights Him? Why or why not?

B. What was the happiest day of your life? Have you ever been so happy that you couldn't express it? You couldn't contain it and you had to scream or cry or jump around.

C. That's the kind of crazy delight the Lord gets about us! He invented holidays (Exodus 23:14)! He looks down at us and loves it when we smile or laugh. Close your eyes and picture God looking at you like that, so happy that you're His daughter, so excited that you're thinking about Him right now. In fact, He's so happy, He starts to laugh out of pure joy. That's how much He loves you!

Day 3

Read Philippians 4:4

A. What does the verse say to do twice? When are we to do it? Why do you think we're commanded to do it twice?

B. "Rejoice" is a cool word. The prefix "re" means to do over or to do again. The root word is joy. The word really means that we need to find our joy again. Have you lost your joy in any area of your life? Have you ever felt like joy was impossible to find?

C. Happiness comes and goes in life, and if we're having trouble finding joy, it's probably because we're missing it completely and looking for happiness instead. Remember that happiness is based on whether or not things are going good. Joy is based in who God is and how He sees us. Make a list of things that make you happy. Now make a list of things that bring you joy. How are the lists different?

DAY 4

Read Romans 8:1

A. What is condemnation? Don't know? Pull the dictionary off the shelf or ask Siri. (No. Wait! That's a terrible idea. I just tried it and Siri told me condemnation is a Welsh Alternative Rock Band. Siri lies. Just google it.) Write down what you find. Why isn't there condemnation for those in Christ Jesus?

B. Have you ever thought about what we, as humans deserve and how Jesus saved us from that? Are you ever tempted to blow off that message because you've heard it before? Why or why not?

C. Make a list of everything Jesus has done for you. The list is endless, but don't stop listing until you catch a glimpse of His love, and are filled with His jo-.

DAY 5

Read Matthew 25:21

A. How does Jesus describe the servant? What is the servant's reward?

B. What is the hardest you ever worked? What was your reward? What did you learn?

C. That's how hard we have to work for our joy. And that doesn't mean we just work hard to get what we want. That's striving after happiness, and it will leave us empty. Working for joy means refusing to let depression and cynicism ruin our day. Because no matter how dark the world gets Jesus is still the Light of the World. No matter how dry our lives become He's still the Living Water. And no matter how depressing life seems He *is* our joy! How are you going to fight for your joy this week?

CHAPTER 7

LIFE: The Roller Coaster

That we should no longer be children,
Tossed to and fro and carried about with every wind of doctrine,
By the trickery of men, in the cunning and craftiness of deceitful
plotting.

EPHESIANS 4:14

Facing the Future

The Best 4.7 Seconds of My Life

I was screaming.

I don't scream very often. Not really my thing.

But that day, I screamed until my vocal chords were thrashed.

That scorching October day, I waited in Southern California sun listening to the screams of hundreds of people as they were plunged one hundred and twenty feet in the air, then plummeted back to the ground. Imprisoned in their seats, they were unable to stop the reeling, or the twisting, or the plummeting.

Only the human brain could think up this kind of cruelty, this kind of torture.

This was California Screaming: The Roller Coaster.

I had dreamed about it all my life. Living on an island in the middle of the Pacific hadn't given me any opportunities for thrilling rides such as this. It was now or never.

But as I listened to the screams of people being launched I wondered why on earth we mortals invent ways to fling ourselves at the sky. I bravely marched on in line and was told to wait at gate four. I took a deep breath, reminding myself that no matter how terrifying the experience was it couldn't last more than two minutes and thirty-six seconds. I pulled the bar down over my head and looked over at my Dad sitting next to me.

He. Loves. Roller Coasters. He turned to me, grinning from ear to ear like he was six years old, and I remembered why I'd strapped myself into this cart of torture; it would be fun. That's right. And I liked fun...didn't I?

Before I could answer my own question the cars started moving. That was the point when I started wondering if I could still turn back. Then the recorded voice came over the speaker. "Not ready? Too bad. Head back. Face forward. And hold on like ya mean it. And away you go in five, four, three, two, ONE!!!"

In 4.7 seconds we went from 0 to 55 mph, and plunged up 12 stories.

At first I couldn't even scream. I was just making sure my stomach was still on my inside. I didn't want to embarrass myself by screaming my head off, but then I looked around, and everyone was screaming. Screaming was even in the name of the Roller Coaster for crying out loud! So I let go and screamed my head off. It was the best 4.7 seconds of my life. In fact, it was the best day of my life so far. (Someday I may get married, and change that last sentence...maybe.)

Get Comfy. There's a Line.

Welcome to The Future; The world's most exciting and terrifying Roller Coaster. Please take a ticket and enjoy. Don't worry about the long line. It will move faster than you think, maybe even faster than you want it to.

In Middle school, it's easy to feel like you've got a long stinky hot line to wait in before the real adventure of your life begins. People always say that the worst part about Disneyland is the lines. They say that you drop all that money to wait in line. For that I have two words: Disneyland App. Two other words to consider are Fast Pass (which is basically a reservation on a Roller Coaster). Honestly in the week I spent in Disneyland there were some extensive lines, but it didn't really matter. We had pretty good timing on most of the rides, but when there was a line, it was nothing to worry about. Because, we were in Disneyland! We played games, took selfies, and just kept saying things like, "Can you believe we're in Disneyland?"

Sadly, you can't get a Fast Pass for life. The nice lady at the counter won't hand you a ticket and say, "Oh, you don't want to wait through middle school? Well you just come back and ten o'clock with that ticket and you can walk right on to high school."

Nope. Not happening. You can't reserve a spot. You can't time it right so that your future comes faster. There's not an app for that. So it's time to wait in line. You get to choose how you wait though. Have you ever seen a person way too impatient to wait in middle school? It's one of the saddest things I've ever seen. Some girls are never satisfied with where they are. When they're eight they want to be ten. When they're ten they want to be thirteen. When they're thirteen they want to be fifteen. It's all in a desire to look grown up, and no one described it better than C. S. Lewis in the final installment of *The Chronicles of Narnia: The Last Battle*.

"'Grown up indeed,' said the Lady Polly, 'I wish she *would* grow up. She wasted all her school time wanting to be the age she is now, and she'll waste all her life trying to stay that age. Her whole idea is to race on to the silliest time of one's life as quick as she can and then stop there as long as she can.'"

Isn't that how we all are sometimes? We don't want to be the age we are. We want to be older, or maybe even younger. We spend so much time trying to be that age that we forget how much fun it can be to wait in line. We complain about the heat, instead of enjoying the sunshine. We complain about the wait instead of taking the time to relax. We complain about the people irritating us instead of enjoying the friends all around us. No one said that waiting in line was easy, but you'll find that the line seems to move quicker if you take the time to enjoy it...and maybe take a selfie.

Think About the Thrill

Don't worry about the hordes of screaming people, or the way the ground beneath your feet trembles when the Roller Coaster's train rumbles by. Don't think about the smell of puke. Think about the thrill. Think about how lucky you are to enjoy this experience. How many in your party? Wait at gate seven. Don't pay any attention to the people who are getting out on the other side of the track. Some of them are laughing. Some of them are crying. Some of them look like they just escaped a Nazi Death Camp. Yeah. Don't look at them.

Waiting in line can also be scary. You see the things that other people on the Roller Coaster have gone through and you wonder if you can handle the future ahead. You hear the screams of the victims of Chemistry homework, feel the rumble of adult responsibilities shaking the ground beneath your feet. You take a deep whiff of the stench of teen age problems and you start to wonder when your stomach learned to break dance. It's in there flopping around doing tricks you didn't know it could do as you prepare to say goodbye to solid ground…and possibly your lunch. It's okay! You're not only going to live through this. It will be thrilling. High school and your teen years will be some of the best years of your life, but you determine how you'll turn out.

If you tell yourself that a Roller Coaster is terrifying, when you get on it you'll be terrified. If you tell yourself that the future will crush you, or that you might not be prepared then you'll live out your youth in fear instead of in freedom. So don't pay attention to the frightening aspects of the future. Worrying about them isn't going to make them any smaller, or prepare you anymore. God isn't going to fling you into your future without preparing you. So trust Him.

Buckle Up

It's your turn. Climb in. Pull the bar down. (A lesson from experience. Pull it down nice and tight, or your head will rattle around in your seat like a pinball when you hit the loop-the-loop.) Arms up. Pull on the yellow strap. Enjoy the ride.

Safety first. Or third…or wherever it fits, I guess.

Seriously though, safety is paramount when it comes to roller coasters, the future, and life in general. If you don't buckle up, you will fall out of the roller coaster. That's simple science. That bar on your seat is there for a reason. If you don't follow the rules, you're going to get hurt, so let's buckle up.

Before you launch, make sure that you bring the Lord down over your life nice and tight. He'll keep you in place, and when your brain feels like a pinball, He'll steady you. If we're not buckled in tight, we're in for a bumpy ride. If we're not buckled in at all, we risk falling out completely. As Ephesians 4:14 puts it, "That we should no longer be children, tossed to and fro and carried about with every wind of doctrine, by the trickery of men, in the cunning and craftiness of deceitful plotting."

It's time to strap in. Because if we're not seeking the Lord, if we're not in His Word and with His people a slight breath of wind could blow us off course. Not to mention a loop-the-loop at 55 mph.

And Away You Go!

God has great plans for us. Honestly, riding a roller coaster is a huge privilege. So is living life! There's a cost involved when you go to a theme park, but it's nothing compared to the price that Christ paid for us when He died on the cross. 1 Corinthians 2:9 isn't just a reason we should rejoice. It's the reason we should sit back and enjoy the ride. Our eyes haven't seen. Our ears haven't heard. Our hearts haven't even imagined what the Lord has in store for us. So as you get ready to enjoy your roller coaster, don't be impatient. Don't be scared. He knows what He's doing. He's got good plans for you. The next 4.7 seconds may be some of the best of your life.

Not Ready?
Too bad.
Head Back.
Face Forward.
And Hold on like ya mean it.
And away you go!
In five, four, three, two, ONE!!!

CHAPTER 7

LIFE: The Roller Coaster
Daily Study Guide

DAY 1

Read Isaiah 43:19

A. What is the Lord doing? What question does He ask in the verse? What new things has He done in your life lately?

B. What was the best 4.7 seconds of your life (or really, just the best day of your life in general)? Was it something you were afraid to do at first?

C. God wants us to try new things! He's always tugging at our heart and expanding our view so that we'll step out of our comfort zone. Pray and ask Him if there's anywhere you need to spiritually step out and try something new. Maybe it's witnessing to a friend. Maybe it's just showing kindness to someone who's lonely. What is He asking you to do?

DAY 2
Read Isaiah 40:31

A. Who will have their strength renewed? What three actions are described in this verse?

B. Describe a time when you had to wait on the Lord. Did it challenge your faith? Were you stronger because of it?

C. Often, middle school is a season of waiting. You're waiting for High School, waiting for car keys, and waiting for love. Today, instead of longing for something you can't have, count your blessings. Make a list, adding to it whenever you think of something new this week. (Maybe there will even be a prize for the person with the longest list!)

DAY 3
Read Ecclesiastes 11:7-8

A. What is sweet and pleasant to the eyes? What is a man supposed to do in all his years? According to the verse, why?

B. Okay, so this verse holds a little bit of doom and gloom, but I love the point! Enjoy all of your years! Because as wonderful as life is, there will be a lot of dark days. So instead of wishing that we were in another season of life, we have to enjoy every wonderful day that's given to us! What are three reasons you're are glad to be alive today?

C. How old are you? And what is the best thing about being this age? Come up with five things you love about the age you are.

DAY 4
Read Proverbs 3:25

A. What two things are we told not to be afraid of?

B. What are you most afraid of in your future? How

much would you pay the Lord to make sure that your fears never come true?

C. God's got you in the palm of His Almighty hand. We don't need to fear what He's got in store because His love for us is so great! But sometimes those fears creep in, and one of the best tricks that I've learned for taking care of those fears is writing them out. On paper they often look silly or ridiculous. So write out those future fears that scare you and give them to the Lord, knowing He's got it all under control. Be really honest with Him. Don't worry. You won't be asked to share these fears with the class.

DAY 5
Read Ephesians 4:14

A. What should we no longer be? What might toss us?

B. It's time to buckle in tight! What truth about God makes you feel secure about life? Have you ever seen anyone blown off course by not believing God is who He says He is?

C. Write down as many truths about God as you can think of. Extra points if you can find the Scriptures that back up your truths!

CHAPTER 8

Chosen for an Adventure

Then He said to them,
If anyone desires to come after Me,
Let him deny himself, take up his cross daily,
And follow Me.

LUKE 9:23

Following Christ

An Unexpected Journey

"I am looking for someone to share in an adventure..."

Those words never fail to give me chills. We all love the idea of an adventure. I think Tolkien phrased it better than anyone when he spoke through the voice of Gandalf. Why do we love that idea? Why are those always our favorite stories? We just feel we have to believe...

That a girl could step through a wardrobe.
That a hobbit could take an unexpected journey.
That a recluse orphan could become a Jedi Master.
That a normal guy could become a super soldier.
That a serving girl could become a princess.
And that someone wants us to share in an adventure.

These are some of the top grossing stories of all time.

We, as humans are fascinated by adventure. We know, however, that adventures don't just happen. We need to be chosen for them. That's why Gandalf's words always give me chills. He chooses Bilbo out of the blue. The pleasure loving hobbit literally lives under a rock, and yet he is sought out and invited to go on an adventure.

We want so much to believe that we're special that we'll pay ten bucks a head at the theater to see someone else who is normal like us be chosen for the adventure of a lifetime. We love the underdog, the hero that really isn't heroic at all. There's no reason in the world that Gandalf or Obi Wan or Aslan should ever have chosen them, but they were chosen, just the same.

So were you.

Jesus Christ waits for you to share in an adventure with Him (John 10:10).
You didn't choose Him, but He chose you (John 15:16).
He planned out your feats of adventure before you were even formed (Ephesians 2:10).
Now He stands at your door and knocks. (Revelation 3:20).
He says, "Follow Me." (John 1:43).
There will be a cost, though (Luke 14:28-29).
When the adventure is finished you will never be the same (1Corinthians 15:51).
You may lose everything (1 John 3:16).
He asks you to deny yourself, pick up your cross, and follow Him anyway (Luke 9:23).
Will you?

The Black Moment

Let me be clear on something. I'm not just talking about salvation. Although that *is* an adventure, God has a much bigger plan for you than just getting you to Heaven. It's easy to be a Christian without going on the adventure Christ has planned in your life. Plenty of Christians are fine with living the easy life. They go to church on Sundays, act like decent people, and read a verse a day to keep the devil away. If you were to ask them they'd say that that's enough for them. But is it enough for you? Do we want to live a safe life, or an adventurous one? It's up to us.

Merriam-Webster defines adventure as "An exciting or dangerous experience." And that about sums it up. Danger's the name of the game.

I write fiction with adventurous twists, and there's a lot to be learned from a decent adventure. When I'm plotting out my story I plan plenty of danger and loss. You see, an adventure needs to form my characters into who I created them to be. That usually means there's some peril involved. I'd say that on average my heroines have at least two or three near death experiences, plenty of enemies, and at least one major loss. Why? Because if I tried to tell you a story about a girl who had a perfect life, a perfect family, and perfect hair you'd fall asleep. I know you want to see a girl who's life is destroyed beyond repair, who must fight for what family she has left, tossing her own wants and messed up hair aside so that she can overcome the odds and win the day. That's what we all want.

So why do we shy away from those things in our own lives? We hate to experience anything unpleasant. The perils that thrill us, the stories we read, and the movies we watch are usually our worst nightmare. When our lives feel destroyed we say, "God, where are you?" When we have family trouble we think, "Why do I have to go through this?" When our hair is messed up we pout that life's so unfair. But when those things come, it's easier to face them knowing that they're part of the adventure.

If we know that the Eternal Author is weaving our story together, then we're willing to walk through the dark chapters of our lives, because they *will* come.

One of the hardest chapters to write as an author is *The Black Moment*. It comes right before the final battle. The hero finally feels like a hero. She's ready to face the villain head on with the bravery that only her trials could have given her. Then everything goes terribly wrong. The villain had an advantage she didn't count on, her friend stabbed her in the back, and someone (usually her closest ally) gets killed. She suddenly stands alone against the villain. She was outnumbered ten to one before. Now it's a hundred to one and she doesn't have a chance. So she gets up and faces the villain anyway, because she's a hero.

Let me tell you something. You weren't just called to be a good little Christian girl. You were called to be a hero.

Even when life feels like it's crashing down on you. Even when all odds are against you. Even when you feel like you stand alone against all the powers of darkness you are called to be a hero. You were meant for so much more than just surviving middle school! You were called to change the world! There will be Black Moments in your life! There will be days when you're so exhausted, so frustrated, or so sad you feel like you can't even get up out of bed in the morning. Then you will because you're a hero.

A Note from the Author

One nice thing about being the author is that I'm in control…usually. I tell the story. I create the characters. I'm in control. How ridiculous would it be for me to be afraid of my own story? What if my own villain made me nervous? What if I was worried that the odds would be too great for my hero to overcome? What if I got to my Black Moment and said, "Oh no! What's going to happen? I hope she makes it out of here alive!" These thoughts don't cross my mind as I write. I created the difficult odds. I allowed the hard times for my characters, knowing that they could overcome them, because I have overcome my story world. I'm stronger than any of my villains. I'm bigger than any of my hero's problems. I'm the author, and if I wanted to I could make those problems disappear.

God is the Author of all our stories. That's not to say that we're just puppets in His story. We have freewill in the decisions we make, but He knows us all so intricately. He has crafted your life better than any author ever could. Our enemies that seem so strong, these odds that seem so great, they're nothing! The Writer of our story has overcome this world! He's not just the Writer. He's also the true hero. He conquered Satan, darkness, and death and invites us to do the same. He doesn't promise it will be easy, but He's in control. It was our Hero Who said, "In this world you will have trouble, but take heart! I have overcome the world." (John 16:33)

We might have trouble, but Jesus Christ is bright even in our blackest moment, stronger than our powerful enemy, and greater than the greatest odds. That's just how He rolls. What have we to fear?

Happily Ever After

So if I didn't make this clear earlier, I think sad endings are stupid. Sad endings are devised by hopeless humans that have a desire to teach us that life doesn't give us happy endings. Well that may be true. Life doesn't offer happy endings, but Jesus does! Think about it. There are no sad endings with Jesus. If we're following Him, we're headed for a happy ending. It's going to be amazing, people!

Just when this world is at its blackest, and hope seems to have faded like a forgotten dream the Hero, Faithful and True will ride in on a white horse (Revelation 19:11).

The enemies of God will gather in all their might (Revelation 19:19).

Christ will speak, and they will be destroyed (Revelation 19:20-21).

Then His Bride, the church will make herself ready, and we will celebrate at the greatest wedding this world has ever seen (Revelation 21:2).

And we'll all live happily ever after (Revelation 21:4).

Tell me that's not the greatest ending ever!!!

So if you're life feels black, if your ending feels sad, it's not the end. It's only the black moment. So get back up! Keep fighting, because the happy ending is coming. We're all going to be there and we'll tell the stories of how our Author weaved together our adventure. I want mine to be a story worth telling. And I can't wait to hear yours!

He's looking for someone to share in an adventure. What do you say?

Chosen for an Adventure
Daily Study Guide

DAY 1

Read John 10:10

A. What does the thief come to do? What did Jesus come to bring us? What do you think it means to have life *more abundantly*?

B. Has Jesus ever called you on an adventure? I'm not talking dragons and light sabers here! Has He ever taken you outside your comfort zone? What happened?

C. We're going to try something a little different this week. You're going to write your own mini-adventure! And don't be scared. There won't even be any real writing assignments. We're just going to develop a story for fun. It can be any genre you want. Historical, contemporary, science fiction, fantasy, you pick! If you're not sure what kind of story you want, what's your favorite kind of story to read/watch? Once you know what kind of story you want to work with, it's time for Step 1:

Create your hero. Make it a girl close to your own age. What does she look like? What's her name, favorite color, and favorite food? Where does she live? What is she most afraid of? What does she want more than anything in the world? How is she like you? How is she different?

DAY 2
Read Luke 9:23

A. What three commands are in this verse? What seems like the hardest one to do? Why?

B. Jesus never sugar coated anything. He tells it the way it is. He didn't ever say to His disciples, "Follow Me and everything is going to be fun! We're never going to work or have difficulties. We're just going to eat candy and relax all the time!" He said we'd have trouble. Why do you think Jesus lets us go through hard times? What's the hardest thing you've ever had to go through for Him?

C. Okay! Time to create a story. Pick three things that your hero will lose in your story. Will it be money, loved ones, safety, security? What will she have to give up before the story is over? What will be the biggest lesson she learns?

DAY 3
Read Genesis 50:20

A. What does God do with the evil that people plan? Why did He do it, according to Genesis 50:20?

B. Have you ever had someone in your life that wanted bad things to happen to you? Did you ever have a friend who purposely humiliated or hurt you? How did God bring about good in that situation? Have you forgiven them? It's important to remember that people aren't our enemies. The only true enemy we have is Satan and we don't need to be afraid of him because Jesus already beat him! Don't let our true enemy get a hold in your life by holding onto bitterness! Forgive because you've been forgiven.

C. Now it's time to craft your villain, your hero's enemy. Maybe it's a dastardly wizard. Or, then again, maybe it's a girl at your hero's school. It depends on your story. (Just a little tip, make your villain the perfect opposite of your hero. If your hero likes kittens, your villain is seeking to wipe kittens from the face of the earth, or maybe your villain's just allergic to cats. If your hero is brave and sweet. Make your villain fearful and nasty. Etc.) Who is it that doesn't want your hero to succeed? Why don't they want her to accomplish her goals? What makes them so angry at your hero? Where will they be at the end of the story? Will your hero defeat them, or turn them around for good in the end?

DAY 4
Read John 16:33

A. What will we have in the world? Should this scare us? Why or why not according to the verse?

B. Is it hard for you to believe that Jesus Christ is bigger than your problems? Don't be afraid to answer honestly. Sometimes our problems and our enemies seem huge, and it's hard to believe that God is still in control. What's a hard situation that's going on in your life right now? What do you think it means that Jesus has already overcome that situation? Does it give you courage to believe that?

C. What will be your hero's blackest moment? What

will she lose? How will she suffer? Why will she want to turn back? What makes her keep going?

DAY 5
Read Revelation 21:4

A. What four things will be no more in Heaven? Why, according to the verse?

B. What are you most excited to see/do in Heaven? Any day, Jesus will come back and snatch us up like the Hero He is, carrying us off to His beautiful happy ending. How does knowing that help us to face hard times? His ending is better than anything we could ever hope for! So whatever you're going through, stick it out! Work hard, and know that in the end, you'll be glad you did.

C. I think it's time for a happy ending! How will your story end? Does she win the day? Does she achieve her dream? Is it everything she hoped it would be? How has she changed? More importantly, how have you changed? You wrote an adventure! Good job! I'm so proud of you!!! So when you worry that your Author has forgotten you, remember your story. And remember that Lord of All Creation is a much better writer than any of us could ever hope to be. He knows your story, your villains, your black moments, but He also knows that you will wage a triumphant war and be the hero He created you to be. Take courage, fellow hero. This story isn't over yet.

Dream Chasers and World Changers

Delight yourself in the Lord
And He shall give you the desires of your heart.

PSALM 37:4

Using Your Dreams to Change the World

Finding a Dream

Okay! Let's go on that adventure! Let's take the leap! Let's go for it!

Where am I going again? What am I supposed to do with my life? When is that adventure going to start anyway? Because I prayed and Gandalf still didn't show up at my door. Isn't that what was supposed to happen? I mean, I want to do great things for God, but I'm just so...me. I want to be that one person that changed the world, but what if I'm not the world changing type? I mean I want to be that young person that was so devoted to God and started doing big things for him before I turned eighteen, but time's a tickin'!

I'm already too old to be that child prodigy whose paintings look better than my photos.

Maybe I could be a child singer like Charlotte Church and blow people away with my...oh wait. She was twelve by the time she was on stage. Too late.

Maybe I could be a gymnast like Gabby Douglas and win two gold medals before I'm...oh wait. Cartwheels make me puke. Stupid cart wheels.

We want to be great. We want to change the world. We just don't know how.

Welcome to the life of a Christian teen. Okay, so maybe it's not just Christian teens that struggle with this, but I think we have it a little harder than the teens of the world here. Why? Because we want (or we should want) God's will for our lives. The kids of the world have been told to follow their heart, and do whatever they want. That's terrible advice by the way. Don't listen to your heart. It's a cheat and a liar. Jeremiah 17:9 says "The heart is deceitful above all things, and desperately wicked; who can know it?" Your heart is going to lead you astray. It's going to tell you what you want to hear, and point you in the wrong direction.

So if we want God's will, that's a start, but how can we hear God's voice to know what His Will is? What if I hear what I think might be God's voice, but it's really just my deceitful heart trying to sound like God's voice? Or, what if I listen to that voice that I think is God's and then it turns out that it isn't God's and I end up lonely and depressed with no one but a cockroach to keep me company?!

Deep breath.

If we signed up for the adventure of a lifetime, we've already completed step one. Giving your life to Christ is the way to start. Handing over all your plans is step two.

Do you have any dreams for the future? And by future I mean your plan for this week, and even the next hour. Give your plans to Him. Imagine placing all of your plans and agendas in the palm of His hand. Now let go. Seriously. Let go. It might be kind of hard to pry those fingers off, but once you do, you'll be free.

Did you let them go? All right, now no taking them back. Leave them right where they are.

Read Your Bible Pray Every Day

And you grow, grow, grow…

One of my favorite verses is Psalm 37:4: "Delight yourself in the Lord and He shall give you the desires of your heart."

Does Jesus delight you?

Does spending time with Him make getting up a half-hour early worth it? Do you talk with Him? I'm not talking about just praying in church or at youth group. Do you talk to Him when no one else is around? Do you ask Him about everything, even the stupid things? Like why our eyes can only see a spectrum of six colors, or why He didn't give us the ability to fly, or where He got the idea for the platypus.

Seriously! You have the ear of the eternal Creator of the Universe. This isn't a game of twenty questions! Ask Him anything you want, because He wants to answer you. Jeremiah 33:3 says He wants to "Show you great and mighty things, which you do not know." So ask Him anything!

Let me ask you something. Have you ever had a friend that only talked to you when they wanted something from you? Doesn't that just sting? It hurts. They don't really want your friendship. They just want what you can give them.

But aren't we that way with God sometimes?

We ignore Him for most of the day until we're in trouble. Even then we just whine about our problems. God isn't our personal assistant. He doesn't take orders from us.

If we want to show Him love we need to just talk to Him like He's our friend. A good friend talks with their bestie about everything and nothing. The good stuff, the bad stuff, the crazy stuff, the funny stuff.

How do you know your parents' voices? You've learned to listen for them. You can hear them laugh in a crowd of people. You can find them by their voice because you've been listening for them all your life. If we're constantly listening for God's voice He's going to speak. And the more we listen, the better we'll be at hearing Him when He speaks to us.

Of course, the best place to hear His voice is in His Word. He speaks through the Scriptures, but sometimes we need that extra word. Something that's special for us. We need that still small voice. If we listen for it every day, then when we need to hear from God, we'll know exactly what to listen for.

Dreaming a Dream

What now? It's time to dream. Did you know that God spends His days dreaming about your future? He has dreams for you! They're to help you not to harm you, to give you a future and a hope (Jeremiah 29:11). So instead of spending our life wandering after our selfish hearts, let's think of it like this. The Lord has gone before you, and placed opportunities and dreams in your path. You have to find them like clues on a treasure hunt. Wouldn't it be sad to get to Heaven and see all of the dreams we missed because we weren't paying attention or because we were following our selfish hearts?

So how do we chase God's dreams? Well what are *your*

dreams?

Now, don't get me wrong. I know I said not to follow your heart, but the beautiful thing is, that when we give our lives and plans to him and learn to hear His voice we're able to listen to His heart. If you're talking with Him all the time, and engrossed in His Word, then you will slowly find that your dreams begin to reflect His dreams.

So what's your dream? If you could do anything for the Kingdom of God, ANYTHING, what would it be? Sometimes we try to put ourselves in boxes where we don't belong. We think that serving God means that we have to move to Nigeria and live in a mud hut. Now, I know people who've done that and they did it because God put that desire in their heart. But what has He put in your heart?

Do you like working with kids?

Do you love music?

Have you always wanted to make movies?

Do you just want to be the best mother and wife you can be someday?

Those are incredible, impacting, world shaking dreams! These are the dreams that change history. And that's where they start, just little sparks of a dream.

Don't be afraid of dreaming the wrong thing. If it's not God's will, He'll make it clear through your heart or through His Word. Another way He will speak to you is through the voices of authority in your life. Maybe your dream doesn't fit into your season of life right now. Or maybe it needs more time and prayer. God gave you your parents and your mentors for a reason. So ask them about your dreams. Ask them to pray for you and listen to their advice on making a Godly decision.

And don't be afraid if you don't know what your dream

is yet, because God wants to give you one. So ask Him. Ask Him for a desire for whatever it is He's called you to do. He wants to blow your mind.

So start dreaming. Dream big. When you know what He wants you to do, go for it! Don't let fear or doubt stop you. Make your life about serving Christ, and your dreams will change the world because that's who we were called to be.

Dream Chasers.

World Changers.

Children of the King.

Dream Chasers and World Changers
Daily Study Guide

DAY 1

Read Jeremiah 17:9

    A. What two phrases describe the heart? How does this differ from what the world say about your heart?

    B. Has your heart ever deceived you? Have you ever felt tricked when your heart led you to do something and it didn't turn out?

    C. How has the advice; "Follow your heart" hurt our generation? Give examples.

DAY 2

Read Psalm 37:5

    A. What two commands are in this verse? What does it mean to *commit your way to the Lord*?

B. Have you given your plans to God? Search your heart and see if there are any desires that you're holding back from Him?

C. The verse says, "And He shall bring *it* to pass." What is your *it*? What is it in your life that you want Him to do?

DAY 3
Read Psalm 37:4

A. What do we delight in? And what will He give us? Has He ever surprised you by giving you the desire of your heart?

B. Here's the thing, Him giving us the desire of our heart doesn't mean He'll give us everything we want. It means He'll give us desires in our heart. And when we delight in Him, we start to want what He wants. His desires become our desires, and He has no problem giving us those things. So have you delighted yourself in the Lord? Is He your best friend? How often do you talk? Is it time to draw closer to Him?

C. Spend some time with the Lord. Go on a walk, or find a place where you can be alone and just talk. Make sure you take your Bible and listen for His voice. Talk to Him about anything that comes to mind. How did it go?

DAY 4
Read Jeremiah 29:11

A. What does God have for us? What don't his plans include? What are they going to give us instead?

B. What opportunities are in your path right now? Do you think God has placed them there?

C. Let's find out! Ask Him. Ask Him about your

opportunities. Get some more time alone with Him and while you're at it, ask if there are any dreams He has for your life. Then spend some time reading His Word and listening for His voice. He'll speak. Just listen.

DAY 5

Read Ephesians 3:20

A. What is God able to do? What is at work within us?

B. So what is your dream? What is it you want to do? Do you have a dream? If you don't, ask Him for one. If you could do one thing, or be one thing for God what would it be? What are your natural interests? If the Lord came to you and said, "You can go any direction with your life and I'm going to bless it." Where would you go?

C. How could you make those dreams happen?

CHAPTER 10

Tough Girls in a Tough World

Have I not commanded you?
Be strong and of good courage;
Do not be afraid, nor be dismayed,
For the Lord your God is with you
Wherever you go.

JOSHUA 1:9

Learning to be a Tough Girl

Toughness

Tough girls.

Those words make some girls want to cheer and others want to shudder. In our culture girls are expected to be tough. We're expected to do everything that boys do, only better. Sometimes, I think we get the idea that girly girls can't be tough, that femininity means weakness.

Untrue.

We're called to be tough. God loves to use tough girls. How do I know this? Well, here are some true stories of how He's used them in the past.

The Last Thread of Hope

One more.

One more day in the town she hated.

One more day trying to keep her family alive.

One more day in a house that was more like a prison.

One more day working a job that was killing her little by little.

One more heartbreak.

One more man that didn't really love her.

One more night to cry herself to sleep.

That was her life. Day after day after day. It didn't help that she was living in a war zone. At any second, her home town could be destroyed by a rival nation that was wiping out everything in its path. When the strangers at her door wanted a place to stay she let them in. She could use the extra cash that they would pay for room and board. Maybe then she could save up enough. Maybe then she could get out of here.

After she had shown the guests to their room the knock on the door made her heart stop. Her hands trembled as she went to open it. The police stood at her door. "The men staying here aren't who they say they are," the officer told her. "They're spies, and we're here to arrest them."

Taking a deep breath, she forced herself to be calm. "They were here," she answered. "I didn't know where they were from, but they headed for the city limits before it got dark. You might still be able to catch them."

As she watched the police disappear down the road, her heart began to pound. This was her chance.

"I know who you are," she told the spies. "I know where you're from, and I know why you're here. You are going to destroy this town, and there's nothing we can do to stop you. Everyone knows it. I will help you get out of here alive, if you swear to spare my family and I."

"We owe you our lives," one of them told her. "If you keep this quiet you and your family will be safe." They gave her a scarlet rope. "Tie this outside your house, and everyone inside will be safe. It will be a sign to every soldier fighting in the attack that it's your house and that we're going to spare you."

Showing the spies the safest escape route, she saved her entire family from a brutal end.

Her name was Rahab, and you can read the rest of her story in Joshua 2.

The girl was tough! She put her own life on the line. If the citizens of Jericho had found out what she was doing they would have put her and her entire family to death. When her city Jericho fell, Rahab and her entire family were saved from the destruction. They were adopted into the nation of Israel. Rahab married a man named Salmon and they had a son named Boaz. We find out in Matthew 1:4 that she was also one of the ancestors of Jesus.

The Death of a Fairy Tale

He was gone.

She was alone. There was no hope left. Not even her cheery, God-fearing mother-in-law could find a silver lining this time. They had lost everything.

"I'm leaving," her widowed mother-in-law announced one day. "I'm going back to my home town."

Without listening to her mother-in-law's protests she packed her bags, leaving her home and everything she'd ever known. Her mother-in-law was a foreigner, but following her to a foreign country was better than living alone.

This wasn't what she had planned. She'd pictured her life when she was a little girl. She would marry a wonderful man who would love her. She would raise their children, but that fairy tale had died when her husband had. Now she had to go get the first job that would take her in order to support herself and her mother-in-law.

She worked hard day after day, doing the best she could at her dead end job. Little did she know, someone was watching.

The CEO of the company watched the young immigrant girl work her hardest. He understood the difficulty of living in a foreign land. His mother Rahab had been a Canaanite woman rescued from the city of Jericho by a scarlet chord. He watched her endurance. The way she toiled to support her family touched his heart. He asked about her. Her name was Ruth. She was from Moab, and her story was just beginning.

Ruth was the real deal! She was the Biblical career woman. Although she had surely planned on a stable life in her homeland she left everything familiar for a country she'd never seen and a God she didn't know. When her dreams died Ruth got back up and kept fighting, and God blessed her. She went on to marry that CEO named Boaz. Together they had baby named Obed who had a son named Jesse who had a son name David, a scrawny red haired kid with an affinity for harp music and giant killing. She's also in Jesus' family line! To read the rest of her story check out the book of Ruth!

The Star of the Show

The smell of the perfume made her sick.

The feel of the silk against her skin made her shudder.

The jewels at her throat were suffocating.

Her stylist assured her she'd do fine. He'd known she

was a star from day one.

Day one had been over a year ago. That's when the madness had started. That was the last day she had been a normal girl. Now she had been entered into the most disturbed beauty pageant of all time. What was the prize? Prince Charming; a man so cruel and self-absorbed that he had sent his last wife packing over a dinner invitation.

After a year of treatment and training she was up.

The country had a new queen.

In one day an orphan girl became the most important woman in the nation. She didn't mention her past to anyone, especially the king. Neither did she mention that she was a Jew. It didn't matter. He didn't ever listen to her anyway. Someone else always had his ear. That someone was his consultant. His right hand. His number two; a man with hatred so deep that he began to make plans to annihilate the Jewish people.

Warned by her cousin of the plot, the queen knew what she had to do.

If she marched in before the king without an invitation the cost would be her life. If she remained silent the cost would be the life of every Jewish citizen in the country. She and her servants prayed and fasted for three days. Assured by her cousin that she had been chosen for such a time as this, she took a deep breath. "If I perish, I perish." With these words she entered the throne room.

Heart pounding, she made her offer to the king; date night. A romantic dinner for…three. The king's consultant was invited as the third wheel. Two nights in a row she put on a lavish feast.

On the second night she found her nerve. "My people and I have been sold like slaves," she told her husband.

He demanded to know who would do such a thing.

She pointed to none other than their dinner guest who faced a cruel end for his conspiracy.

Queen Esther goes down as the toughest girly girl in the book! She saved an entire race by her courageous beauty. She was quite literally a warrior princess, and one of my heroes.

Femininity's Strength

And there are so many more!

Moses' mother had faith enough to put her baby in a basket in the Nile River! (Yeah, snakes, crocodiles. Apparently there were issues with the local daycare.)

Hannah was willing to give up her firstborn son.

And Mary could say the words, "Let it be to me according to Your will." When she knew that God's will could have gotten her stoned in the street.

Tough! Girls!

God uses tough girls. I think our only problem is we have the wrong definition of tough. In a culture that confuses beauty with body image, and femininity with weakness we're easily messed up. What is femininity? The simplest definition is "Being a girl." *Feminine* is almost a taboo term today. Girls dress and act like guys to prove they're not weak. There's just one problem with that. We have nothing to prove. Women are just as tough as men. Case in point? Childbirth. No questions? Good.

Girls are tough. God made us that way, but He also gave us a different job than the guys. We're the sensitive ones, the lovers of beauty, the nurturers. It's how we're designed. It's not anything to be ashamed of, or disguise.

We're meant to be feminine. That doesn't mean we can't love sports or work hard or wear pants for crying out loud! But we need to be content with who God created us to be, and not wish we were someone else.

We're buying into a lie if we think;

A tough girl is the kind of girl who enjoys violence.

A tough girl is the kind of girl who can catch a football better, work harder, and bench more than the average guy.

A tough girl is the kind of girl that wins the Hunger Games.

Untrue.

A tough girl is the kind of girl that puts others' needs before her own.

A tough girl is the kind of girl who knows what she believes and isn't ashamed of it.

A tough girl is the kind of girl who presses on in life, no matter how hopeless her situation seems, or how impossible her life feels.

A tough girl is the kind of girl who doesn't worry about tomorrow, but let's tomorrow worry about itself.

A tough girl is the kind of girl who is strong for the ones around her, but let's herself cry.

A tough girl is the kind of girl who isn't afraid to ask for help, or to give it.

A tough girl is the kind of girl who lays down her life day after day, knowing that she is doing what God has called her to do.

And that's the kind of tough girls you and I are called to be.

Tough Girls in a Tough World
Daily Study Guide

DAY 1

Read Joshua 6:23-25

    A. What three words would you use to describe Rahab? (If you don't remember the rest of her story, check out Joshua 2!) Why do you think God chose to use her?

    B. What do you think it means to be a tough girl who is still feminine? What does it look like to be a girl that's tough for God?

    C. Name three women that you know who are tough for God. Remember, they don't have to be superheroes or anything! Who do you consider to be a woman with a tough faith? Do they know how much you admire them? You should let them know!

Day 2

Read Ruth 1:16-17

A. What did Ruth promise Naomi? How did this show bravery and strength in Ruth's character?

B. Ruth's toughness didn't show in battle or in stubbornness. She was tough by taking care of her family. Sometimes being gentle and tenderhearted and taking care of those we love is the tough thing God is calling us to do. Have you ever seen this in your own life or somebody else's?

C. What tough thing is God calling you to do right now? What is an area where you need to be a tough girl? Write a prayer for His strength in this area of your life.

Day 3

Read Judges 4:14-15

A. What was Deborah's job? Where was her office? What did the children of Israel come to her for?

B. Deborah spoke for God when no one else would. Have you ever felt like the only one who would take a stand for God? What happened?

C. God brought victory because Deborah listened to Him. Spend some time listening for God's voice today. Is there anything He's telling you to do?

Day 4

Read Esther 4:14-16

A. According to Mordecai, why had Esther come to the kingdom? What was Esther's response?

B. Have you ever been afraid to do the right thing because it was unpopular? What happened?

C. Be listening this week to see if there is anything the Lord wants you to say. It might be to encourage someone, or to let someone know that you're praying for them. Speak life this week and be ready to share how the Lord used you.

DAY 5
Read Joshua 1:9

    A. What has God commanded you? Why?

    B. Who is your favorite Bible heroine? Why?

    C. What does it mean to be a tough girl? We're called to be courageous and tough! Don't be afraid, dear one! Be of good courage! The Lord your God is with you wherever you go.

CHAPTER 11

Warriors
(And All the Tough Girls Said, "Amen!")

Therefore take up the whole armor of God
That you may be able to withstand in the evil day,
And having done all to stand.

EPHESIANS 6:13

Fighting in a Spiritual War

Welcome to the Battlefield

We're going to play a game. It's called "Fill in the Blank." I want you to fill this blank with the first negative word that comes to mind. Ready?

Teenagers are the most _____ people.

What words came to my mind? Distracted. Destructive. Disturbed. Depressed. Desperate.

Why?

We can blame our society. We can blame pop culture. We can blame the government, the school system, or even ourselves, but that's not the problem.

Most people would tell you, "Teens are just that way! It's who they are."

It was a teen that slew a giant (1 Samuel 17). It was a teen that gave birth to the Messiah (Luke 2). It was a teen that held onto his faith in Babylon (Daniel 1). It was a teen that was taken to Egypt as a slave, and still believed God was good (Genesis 39).

Teens can be the most energetic, the most passionate, the most powerful people group in the Body of Christ.

And Satan knows it.

So where are the Davids? Where are the Marys? Where are the Daniels and the Josephs? We're in a war! Where are the warriors?

Mary would have showed up today, but she looked in the mirror and felt ugly and unusable.

David's here. He's on the battlefield, but while shells explode around him he's staring at a screen that plays images of espionage, the program of the enemy, meant to steal, kill, and destroy him.

Daniel's around here somewhere, but he's so scared. He can hear the roaring lion that is our enemy, and it renders him useless. So he flies under the radar. No one's really sure what side he's on.

And as for his friends Shadrach, Meshach, and Abed-Nego, they tried to stand up to that idol, but their peers all cracked under the pressure, and even the adults in their life told them, "It's what all young people do."

Esther is here too, but that crush of hers may as well be a king, because he rules her heart. She knows it's wrong. She knows he isn't the right one, but she can't say no because she can't bear the break up. She's so afraid of being alone.

Where are they? They're here. They're slowly being lulled to sleep by the lies.

And I, for one, am done watching it happen.

Girls, it's fun to talk about chocolate and fuzzy socks and lipstick, but the reality is we were born onto the battlefield. We have a very real enemy who wants to take us out. So it's time to buckle down. Welcome to the battlefield.

Take a uniform and a sword and get ready to march, because we have a war to win!

It's Just…

Don't freak out on me! I know that's a lot to take in, but if we're going to live the great story Christ has written for us we have to understand something. In chapter one you introduce the hero. In chapter two you introduce the villain. Why? Because every time you take a stand for something, you will face opposition.

As Winston Churchill said, "You have enemies? Good. That means you've stood up for something, sometime in your life."

When we take a stand on the Word of God, Satan wants to take us out. Don't be scared by this! Our Creator has overcome the world, remember? He already won the war, and we just get to fight in His name! He overcame Satan and death when He rose again. It's over, and Satan knows it.

Here's the catch though; the devil is just about every evil thing you can imagine, but he's not stupid. If he showed up in front of us, looking all evil we'd run to God or we'd pray or we'd quote Scripture, which would render him utterly defeated. Our enemy is way too smart to offer us a vile, boiling cup of green sin. He knows we wouldn't fall for that. Instead he offers us a harmless slice of temptation, just like he offered Eve. That's the thing about sin. It looks so harmless. It's just this once. It's just between us. It's just my little escape.

It's just sin. And we can't play around with it. It's time to wake up and see that people are perishing all around us from tasting that fruit. Even good Christian kids are being taken out by the enemy!

It's easy to grow scared. *What if that happens to me? What if I do the terrible things that they do? I don't think I would, but I didn't think they would either, and look at them!*

It's easy to grow apathetic. *Oh, that's just how kids are. You can't change it. That's just life.*

We don't need to be fearful, but we can't let it just go by either. So what do we do?

First we need to make sure we're okay. Are we in the Word of God? Are we in communication with Him? Do we have strong Christians in our lives who will guide us to walk in His ways?

When we know that our relationship with God is good, it's time to look around at the wounded, the hurt, and the dying. They need Jesus! "And on some have compassion, making a distinction; but others save with fear, pulling them out of the fire, hating even the garment defiled by the flesh." (Jude 1:22-23)

Our brothers and sisters are falling all around us. I don't want to get to Heaven and find out that someone I knew, who went to my church, who was a friend of mine walked without the Lord, and I didn't even notice. We are called to so much more than that!

Suit Up

So it's time to get down to business. We're going to war. Let's put our armor on.

"Put on the whole armor of God that you may be able to stand against the wiles of the devil." (Ephesians 6:11)

What's first? The Belt of Truth. If we really believe in God's truth, it's at our center and nothing can steal it from us.

Next the Breastplate of Righteousness. One of the enemy's favorite games to play is trying to get us to doubt our standing in Christ. He wants nothing more than to make us believe that God is angry at us. Never forget that you are precious in the sight of our Lord and that He has clothed you in the blood of His Son. If there is sin our life we need to confess it, repent of it, and be delivered from it. If we can't "lay aside the sin which so easily ensnares" we won't be able to "run with endurance the race set before us" (Hebrew 12:1). Being in sin holds us back from our destiny. Ain't nobody got time for that!

Shoes of Peace. Everywhere you go you are to take His peace with you. This is so cool! It's a two for one! Because it means that wherever you go He will give you peace, and you will also have the power to give His peace to others.

The Shield of Faith. Yeah, this is important. Paul says to grab this piece of your armor, "Above all…" That means it's serious. Why is it so important? Because Satan doesn't have the guts to fight you with a sword. He knows you are filled with the living power of Jesus Christ. So he shoots arrows at you. Ephesians 6:16 calls them "fiery darts." The only thing that can quench them is your faith. When you really believe that God is Who He says He is, and you are Who He says you are, nothing the enemy throws at you can singe you.

Secure your Helmet of Salvation. Knowing that nothing, nothing, nothing can separate you from Christ is what protects your mind from the blows of this world. Salvation is final. It's secure. If you belong to Christ you are safe for all of eternity.

And The Sword of the Spirit which is the Word of

God. It's our greatest weapon. The rest of the armor is what we use to defend ourselves, but the sword is what we use when we want to go on the offense. Memorizing Bible verses is the simplest, yet most powerful spiritual defense I know of. If you don't have time, make time. If you need to use a trick, use one. For me, Bible verses don't stick in my mind as well as they should, so my family has always memorized them to songs. Does it sound weird? Yes. We have passages set to every tune from *Rolling in the Deep* to *Do you want to Build a Snowman*. We sound crazy, but as a result we have hundreds of verses memorized. Whatever works!

There are days when I wake up exhausted. I know the day ahead is going to be a battle. I know it's going to be hard. So I recite Ephesians chapter 6 before my feet even hit the floor. Before anything else starts I imagine putting on my armor, and you know what? It's never failed me.

You're Not the One Who Should Be Scared

I'm not trying to scare you. The last thing we need as Christians is to be afraid of the devil. We *do* need to realize how afraid he is of us.

He is terrified that you'll listen to the Lord.

He is afraid that you'll never fall for his trap.

He is scared to death that you'll dream your dreams for Christ.

And the thought that you might possibly lead others to Christ makes his knees go weak.

That's how powerful you are. That is the kind of girl you were meant to be. So don't hang out on the side lines. Jump into the battle unafraid, because Christ has already won the war, but He wants us to know what it feels like to slay giants and conquer the powers of Hell. So let's get our armor on and start marching.

I may never march in the infantry
Ride in the cavalry
Shoot the artillery
I may never fly over the enemy
But I'm in the Lord's army
Yes Sir!

Warriors
(And All the Tough Girls Said, "Amen!")
Daily Study Guide

DAY 1

Read 1 Timothy 4:12

A. What shouldn't people despise you for? What should we be instead? In what six categories should we be an example?

B. Have you ever seen young people that stepped up for God? Who were they? What did they do? What are three ways the enemy tries to trip up young people?

C. It's so easy to think that we can only do important things for God when we're adults, but what could you do for God while you're still young? It doesn't have to be huge. What little things could you do to serve God right now?

How is the enemy trying to discourage you from doing them? Pray for strength, courage, and direction as you move forward into what God has for you.

DAY 2
Read 1 Corinthians 10:13

A. No temptation had overtaken you except what? What will God not allow? What will He always make?

B. Time for a diagnostic. How are you doing with the Lord, really? When was the last time you and Him talked? How often are you in His Word? Is there anything keeping you away from Him? Spend some time with Him! We need to constantly center ourselves on Him. If we don't, our walk with the Lord is a pure adrenaline rush from one place to the next, or maybe it's a lazy stroll across the battlefield. Either one is dangerous! We need to be in constant communication with our Captain if we're going to conquer the battles ahead of us.

C. Now what about those around you? Is there a fellow warrior in need of encouragement? Or maybe a lonely sister in need of a friend? It's scary out here on the battlefield, and we need each other. What about those being held captive by the enemy? Are there any non-believers who need your prayers?

DAY 3
Read Ephesians 6:10-13

A. What should we be strong in? Why? What are we wrestling against? So what should we take up?

B. What do you think it means to be strong in the Lord? What is "the power of His might?" What has God done in your life to show you His power?

C. What does it mean to stand like it talks about in verse 13? Have you ever taken a stand for Jesus Christ? Is there anywhere He's calling you to take a stand now?

Day 4
Read Ephesians 6:14-17

A. How many pieces of armor are in the armor of God? What are they?

B. In case you're having trouble grasping the symbolism, let's break it down:

- *Believing God's truth*
- *Being confident that you are right before Him*
- *Knowing that His peace goes with you always*
- *Having faith that everything He says is true*
- *Knowing you have received His salvation through grace*
- *Knowing and believing what His Word says*

These are the pieces of the armor of God. Which one is hardest for you to really take hold of and "put on?"

Day 5
Read James 4:7

A. What two commands are given in this verse? What will the result be if we obey them?

B. Which one of the commands sounds harder for you? Why?

C. "Greater is He Who is in you than He Who is in the world." (1 John 4:4) The war is won! The battle is ours to take if we only obey! Satan is very real and very powerful and he hates you very much, but don't be afraid! He's trembling in his boots, because guess who opened her Bible today? You're searching the Word. You're spending time in prayer, and he's absolutely sick to his stomach about it. So don't worry about him. You just keep doing what you do for Christ. Submit to Him. Resist the devil. And, honey, he's gonna flee. It might be a fight. It might be a battle. But we're right here in the trenches with you, standing against our powerful enemy by the grace of our Lord Jesus Christ Who has made us more than conquerors. So put on your armor! And stand! We are the warriors of the Kingdom. So go kick butt! And I mean that in the most spiritual way possible. ;)

CHAPTER 12

Your Story

You are writing a gospel, a chapter each day
By deed that you do, by words that you say
Men read what you write, whether faithless or true
Say, what is the gospel, according to you?

AUTHOR UNKNOWN

Sharing Your Testimony

Testimony Night

A circle of chairs is positioned in the room. You glance around nervously, wondering if everyone else is as unprepared as you are. They don't seem to be. To everyone else this seems like just one more church event. They couldn't possibly understand why your palms are sweating or why you constantly glance at the clock. No one quite feels the pressure like you do. No else quite understands the terror of *Testimony Night*.

Have you ever been there? If not, allow me to shed some light on this bane of Christian kid existence. You sit in a circle and one by one everyone tells their testimony of how they came to know Christ. There's just one problem; you don't remember how you came to Christ. Or maybe you remember, but it's nothing to report. Most Christian Kid testimonies go something like this:

"I was four years old. My mommy said, 'Do you want

to go to Heaven?' I said, 'Yes.' Then Mommy told me I needed to believe in Jesus and ask Him to live in my heart, so I did. And now I'm here. The end." That doesn't sound too bad until you hear the other testimonies floating around the room.

"Well…" one man sighs as he leans back in his chair." I was on drugs, in and out of jail, living like a rat, and then I found Jesus."

Another woman starts in, "I was a single parent, with no way to make the rent and suddenly this stranger gave me a check and said, 'Jesus loves you.' I think she was an angel. I went home and got saved."

"I was dying of cancer and the Lord healed me miraculously."

"I was wealthy, then lost everything and had to turn to Jesus."

"I was a Satan Worshiper."

"I had demons cast out of me."

"I was on death's door."

"Then I found Jesus."

As they go around the circle you begin to sink lower in your seat. Their testimonies are awesome. Theirs is like an epic blockbuster with action scenes, plot twists, and peril. Yours is like a comic strip in the Sunday morning paper. Not the cool kind. The sad kind.

You suddenly feel about three inches tall in a room full of spiritual giants. You just want to wrap up your cheap little testimony and go home.

Then it's your turn. By now you're wondering if you're even saved, and the words tumble out one on top of the other. "I…you know…believe in God." *No wait, that sounds stupid.* "I mean I don't really remember, but you know, I

144

know it happened so…yeah, I'm saved." *Or at least I thought I was until tonight.* "I'm going to Heaven. I love Jesus and all that." *Holy cow! A tree stump has a better testimony than me.*

Fear not! The Testimony Blues are not yours alone to bear. You have a testimony, and it's time to pull it out and use it. Because your story is one of the greatest gifts you've been given.

*Test*imonies

So maybe that's not you. Maybe you have a great testimony of when you first realized that God was real, and that His Son Jesus Christ paid for your sins, and rose from the dead. If you do, that's great! But I think no matter what our testimony is we have trouble sharing it. We think it's not important, or we just don't like to talk about it in front of other people.

I think one of the biggest misunderstandings is that we think a testimony has to be the story of when we got saved. If that story isn't impressive we feel like we don't have one.

It's dangerous to believe this, because that opens the door to Christian kids thinking that have to create a testimony. I've heard Christian kids say that they have to go get into trouble, and hang with the wrong crowd before they'll have a real testimony. They want the gnarly testimony. But let me tell you something, being a child of the One True King who's not interested in the things of this world, *is* an incredible testimony of God's power! Think about it! You might be the only kid in your school or maybe even the only kid your church who has a great relationship with the Lord. Don't throw that away!

As for me, I have the classic Christian Kid Testimony. I

don't remember saying a prayer, but I know I was about three years old when Jesus entered my life. When I was eight, I freaked out and thought I might not be saved because I couldn't remember ever saying the Sinner's Prayer. I recommitted my life to Christ, and got baptized. It's that simple, but when I'm called upon to share my testimony that's not what I share. Because a testimony is just a story of when God changed your life whether that was ten years ago, or yesterday. Whether it was when you got saved, or when you just learned to treat people with kindness. When God moves in your life you have a testimony.

My testimony is something God has done in my life in the last few years. Like I said, I've been a Christian since I was three. I've grown up in church. I've been baptized. But my testimony isn't about when I found my faith. It's about when my faith was tested.

Our family had gone through a rough couple of years. Starting from the time I was thirteen we seemed to lose one loved one after another. We'd also lost friendships and nights of sleep and my mom's health was suffering as a result. It was one of those rough season that everyone has now and then. The season had gone on for three years, and one day I just couldn't take it anymore. My mom had come to me, looking tired and dazed from a miserable week.

"I don't know," she said, staring off into space like someone had knocked the wind out of her. "We're just so tired. The ministry is just really tough right now, and it's hard on our family."

It was the most discouraged I had ever seen her and my heart was breaking because there was nothing I could do. When she left my room, I curled up on my bed and cried my eyes out. I was angry at God. I didn't understand how He could let this happen. Hadn't we served Him? Hadn't we done everything He'd ever asked? Why had He allowed so many trials in our lives?

When I had cried all my tears, I didn't move. I watched as the sun dipped down toward the horizon. Then a thought came to me; I could fake this. I didn't have to be the Super Christian. I could just be the everyday, go to church on Sunday Christian. I could keep the ministry, and the Lord and arm's length and just be a normal person. I knew how to look really spiritual. I knew how talk the walk. I could fake it.

Then the Lord's voice came to my heart so soft and gentle, yet so clear. "Am I still good?" He asked.

I didn't want to answer. I was still angry at Him.

"Am I still good?"

"Lord, these people!"

"Am I still good?"

"But my circumstances!"

"Am I still good?"

"Lord, everything You've allowed in my life. Why?"

"Am I still good?"

I knew the answer. It formed in my heart, then in my mind, then on my lips. "Yes." He was still good.

I'd like to say that I fell to my knees, and felt a rush of the Holy Spirit's joy at that very moment, but I didn't. I got up, and I washed my face, and I took whatever step was next, knowing that life would be hard, that being a Christian would not be easy, and that my will wasn't always God's will. But I also knew that He was good. I knew that my life would be empty if I tried to push Him away, and every day since I've tried to draw closer.

Our Stories

That's my testimony. My story. I was already saved, but that was when I didn't just *believe* that God was real. I *knew* He was. He wants us all to have that experience, to really know He's there. That's why He lets us go through hard things! That's why He tests us. Because if we're not tested we won't have a *tes*timony.

And if you haven't had that moment when you know that you know that God is in the room with you, then ask Him for it.

"And you will seek Me and find Me when you search for Me with all you heart." (Jeremiah 29:13)

He's waiting for you to ask, and if you're having a tough time right now, if you struggling with doubt that's right where He wants to meet you. Middle school is so important. It's the age of decision. It's when we decide who we are and what we believe. So I don't take your story lightly. No matter how silly it sounds, or how simple it is, it's powerful.

One of my favorite verses is in Revelation 12. When we're all in Heaven, at the throne of God, Satan will be cast out of Heaven. A mighty voice will proclaim: "…the accuser of our brethren, who accused them before our God day and night, has been cast down. And they overcame him by the blood of the Lamb and by the word of their testimony …" (Revelation 12:10-12)

The blood of Jesus Christ is the most powerful precious weapon formed against the enemy. Right behind that, is our testimony.

So we need to know! We need to be sure of our testimony, and believe it with all our hearts, because it has the power to overcome the devil and to lead others to Christ. You're living it right now!

So what is your story? When did you know that God was real? When was your faith tested, and how did you overcome?

The world is watching. They're watching you and me to see if this whole "Living for Christ" thing is everything we say it is. They might never walk into a church. They might never read a Bible, but they're watching you. It's been said that you're the only gospel some people will ever read.

So what is the gospel according to you?

Sister, I can't wait to hear your story, whether it's here, or in Heaven. In Heaven, we're having a huge slumber party at my place! Just us girls, and I'm going to hear every one of your stories. I can't wait! So we'd better start practicing! Your story is something no one can ever take away from you. So cherish it, and live it out every day. I love you so much! And I'm so proud of you. Thanks for joining me on this journey. It was just lovely, just us girls.

CHAPTER 12

Your Story
Daily Study Guide

DAY 1

Read Matthew 5:14

A. What are you? What can't be hidden? Why does this verse compare us to a city?

B. What does it mean to you that your life is a gospel? What would your life look like if every day you lived you told God's story with your actions?

C. Saint Francis once said, "Preach the Gospel always. When necessary use words." What are three actions you could do this week that would let people know that you are living Christ without using words? Write them down and do them! Be prepared to share how they went.

DAY 2
Read Hebrews 11:15

A. Who is this verse about? (In case you're wondering this guy's story is amazing! You can find it in Genesis 5:24. He walked with God and "was not" Translation: He's having His morning devotions and poof! Vanishes Houdini style, is taken directly up into Heaven, and never sees death. Am I the only one that's totally geeking out about that?!) What was Enoch's testimony?

B. What have you done in your life that pleased God? Have you ever felt like you were the only one trying to please Him? What was that like? Tell about a time when you didn't want to please God, but you did anyway.

C. This is how we discover our testimony! It might not seem like a big deal, but these stories are what we come back to when our lives feel uncertain and scary. Remembering the times when we stood up for Christ and He didn't let us go, is what we will need to face any struggles that arise. So how did pleasing God draw you closer to Him and how did it change your life?

DAY 3
Read Luke 21:12-13

A. What two things will the enemies of God do? Who will Christians be brought before? What will those terrible times turn out to be?

B. Okay! So don't freak out on me here! I'm pretty sure that you're not in danger of being tossed in prison and led before kings because of your faith. At least not yet anyway. There is persecution going on all over the world, though! We are so blessed in our country to have the freedom to live for Christ, but we still suffer. We still face trials and hard times and persecution of a different kind. What is the hardest thing you've ever gone through? How were you hurt by it? Did you question God's goodness?

C. When you've answered all the questions above, you should have the outline of a decent *testi*mony. God is going to test our faith, allow hard times and then give us the strength to bear them. Just one question left to answer: How did He turn it all around for good? (If you're in the middle of a dark time, don't lose heart! You're going to make it. If it's not happy, it's not the ending! Instead, share what God is doing in the middle of this trial if you are able to do so.)

DAY 4
Read Jeremiah 29:13

A. What three commands are in this passage? How are we to obey them? What would that look like?

B. Have you ever had an experience that showed you that God was real? Have you ever felt His presence? Has He ever made Himself so real to you that you could never deny the power of His existence?

C. Maybe you haven't had that experience. Maybe you're wondering about salvation. If you are, let me tell you something, I am praying that God is going to make Himself so real to you that you'll know from this point on that Jesus Christ is the Son of God, that He loves you, and that He died for your sins. (If you want to know more about how to become a Christian, or what it means to follow Christ, flip to the back of the book.) Maybe you're already saved, but you're starting to wonder if you really believe all of this. I'm praying for you too! I know what it's like to have a moment (Or a week!) of doubt and wonder where God is. Don't give up, sister! He wants to speak to you! You just need to listen, and pray for His Spirit to overcome you and empower you to believe. It might be a slow process, but I promise He'll show up.

DAY 5
Read Revelation 12:11-12

A. Who is the accuser of the brethren? What does he do day and night? How are we to overcome him?

B. Have you ever overcome a temptation or an inner difficulty (i.e. anxiety, depression, self-hate, or lust)? How did God deliver you? (Please remember to not share names and keep it clean. Give God the glory. Don't make it gory.)

C. I hope this week's homework has helped you find your testimony! God does so much in our lives sometimes it all starts to blend together and we start to forget the powerful events of the past! So now the million dollar question: What is your testimony? Ah! I'd give anything to see your answer, but wait! We live in the 21st century! So here's your assignment: Type out your testimony, and send it to me (hannahdugganauthor@gmail.com)! I want to know! I want to hear the powerful gospel Jesus Christ is writing in your life. I want to know what you've gone through and overcome. We need each other! You know my story. Don't deny me the privilege of knowing yours. Even if you don't, I'm praying for you. I love you So my sister!

Having many things to write to you,
I did not wish to do so with paper and ink:
But I hope to come to you and speak face to face,
That our joy may be full.
2 JOHN 1:12

If You Don't Know Jesus

Just Us Girls is designed to build you in your faith and encourage you as you walk with God, but I know that some of you who are reading it do not know Jesus Christ as your personal Savior. I know this because I have prayed for you, prayed that God would put this book in your hands so that you can find out Who He is.

This Bible study is full of advice, tips, and ideas that help us to live Godly lives, but you know what? They are all pointless if Jesus Christ is not the Lord of your life. Without Him it doesn't matter, because without Him we can't find our true identity, we can't possess true joy, and we can't truly live out our destiny. It doesn't matter how good we are. We've all fallen short of God's glory (Romans 3:23). We all need forgiveness.

I don't know where you're coming from. Maybe you've never set foot in church. Maybe church is your life. Maybe you are desperate to find faith. Maybe you're a church kid who's wondering if you really believe this thing. Whoever you are I want you to know that Jesus Christ loves you with an everlasting love.

No matter who you are.

No matter what you've done.

No matter who has hurt you in the past.

No matter how many times you've heard it.

He loves you. He took special care as He created you. He's watched you as you've struggled and stumbled. He holds your every tear in the palm of His hand. He thought of you with His dying breath.

He doesn't want us to handle life on our own. We can't do this without Him, and He knows that. Faith is all about letting go and putting our hope in a God Who has promised to catch us.

Nothing else in life will ever fulfill us; not money, not fame, not romance. He is everything we long for.

If you would like to give your life to Jesus Christ today, just tell Him. Not sure what to say? This is something called the sinner's prayer. These aren't magic words. They simply cover the basics.

Dear Jesus,

I know that I'm a sinner. I've made mistakes. I know that I don't deserve to go to Heaven, and that nothing I could ever do could make me worthy. I believe that you are God. I believe that You died to pay for my sins, and I believe that You came back from the dead. Thank You for loving me. Do whatever You want with my life. It's Yours now.

In Jesus Name, Amen.

I so wish I could be there with you. I wish I could pray with you, but I want to hear your story. I want to know if you prayed that prayer. We are sisters in Christ now, and I am so excited to welcome you into this family! Please send me an email at hannahdugganauthor@gmail.com. Let me rejoice with you. I love you dearly!

ACKNOWLEDGMENTS

Special thanks to the many women in my life who led me by the example of their faith. Your names are too many to mention, but know that I was watching as you fought the good fight a little further down the road.

To my mom, Candie. Your constant love, instruction, and prayer brought me through every difficulty and trial! Thank you for starting a class for just us girls when I was in middle school. I know better than anyone how many times the enemy has tried to knock you down, but watching you taught me how to get back up. I love you so much!

To Darien Gee for editing, opening my eyes to the world of non-fiction, and for showing me what I'm capable of.

To my girlies!!! Olivia, Caitlin, Peyton, River, Tierney, Tatianna, and Morgan, you have been my guinea pigs. For that I apologize. Without you there would be no *Just Us Girls*. It is written to every single one of you. No eye has seen, no ear has heard what God has in store for you! I can't wait to see what it is!

To my faithful Lord Jesus, for teaching me the lessons of these twelve chapters over and over and over again. May I never stop learning. Breathe Your life into these pages. Fill in all the blanks. To You be the glory. Amen.

Scripture References

Chapter 1: Who the Heck Am I?
Scriptures:
Jeremiah 1:5
Psalm 51:10
Ephesians 5:1

Chapter 2: Drama: Did I Sign Up For This?
Scriptures:
1 Thessalonians 4:11

Chapter 3: Best Friends For—Almost—Ever
Scriptures:
Proverbs 18:24
Colossians 2:2
Proverbs 6:3
Proverbs 17:17
Proverbs 22:11
Proverbs 27:6
Proverbs 27:10a
Proverbs 27:17
John 15:13

Chapter 4: The Love of Your Life
Scriptures:
Jeremiah 31:3
Song of Songs 8:4
Psalm 27:4

Chapter 5: Beauty and the Best
Scriptures:
1 Peter 3:3-4
Psalm 139:14

Chapter 6: Fighting Hard For Joy
Scriptures:
Philippians 4:4
1 Corinthians 2:9

Romans 8:1

Chapter 7: LIFE: The Roller Coaster
Scriptures:
Ephesians 4:14

Chapter 8: Chosen for and Adventure
Scriptures:
Luke 9:23
John 16:33

Chapter 9: Dream Chasers and World Changers
Scriptures:
Psalm 37:4
Jeremiah 17:9

Chapter 10: Tough Girls in a Tough World
Scriptures:
Joshua 1:9

Chapter 11: Warriors (And All the Tough Girls said, "Amen!")
Scriptures:
Ephesians 6: 13
Jude 1:22-23
Ephesians 6:11

Chapter 12: Your Story
Scriptures:
Jeremiah 29:13
Revelation 12:10-12

Hannah Duggan is a young woman fervent about God's grace and His will for the young people of this generation. As a worship leader, dance instructor, and Bible study leader, she is constantly pouring into the lives of young people. Her passion for writing stems from her desire to spread the powerful gospel message through both fiction and non-fiction. She has two younger brothers and is an active part of her parents' ministry at Calvary Chapel Hamakua on the Island of Hawaii.

To learn more about Hannah, her books, and her ministry visit www.hannahrosed.com.

Or write her at hannahdugganauthor@gmail.com.

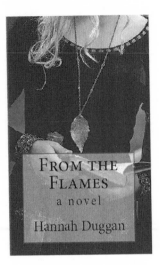

FROM THE FLAMES
a novel

He says he's come looking for her. Her parents suspect him. Her Uncle despises him, but when he offers her writing lessons, fifteen-year-old Elizabeth Atlee never suspects that Peter Lockton is being hunted down as a heretic for translating the Scriptures. As his enemies approach Peter escapes to protect Elizabeth, but too late. Elizabeth's home burns to the ground. In a world of lies and secrets, can she discover God's truth?

DEAR KATE

a novel

At a time when thousands are fleeing tyranny to find a home in the New World, seventeen-year-old Kate Elyot witnesses a tragic accident that orphans a little girl named Emily. Suddenly the sole guardian of a child she's never met, Kate's only guide to the girl's surviving family is a signet ring and a letter addressed "To Kate." Unsure of whether she has walked into a fateful calling or a fatal coincidence, Kate is determine to get Emily home but is unprepared for the journey awaiting her.

Captain Anthony Scot will not rest until his enemy Simon Cephas is punished for a crime long forgotten. The signet ring that Emily carries is the evidence Scot needs to convict his rival. He is willing to obtain the ring at any cost in order to destroy Cephas.

Can Kate fight to free Emily from those who would use her to destroy her Puritan family? Will her courage sustain her as she is brought face to face with her worst fears, deepest regrets, and a God she cannot bring herself to trust?